Y0-BGF-456

OUTDOOR GUIDE

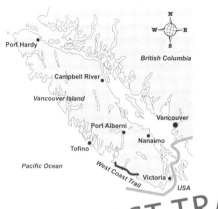

WEST COAST TRAIL

POSITIVE CONNECTIONS LTD

Distributed by
Gordon Soules Book Publishers Ltd.
1359 Ambleside Lane,
West Vancouver, BC, Canada V7T 2Y9
books@gordonsoules.com
604-922-6588 Fax: 604-922-6574

Library and Archives Canada Cataloguing in Publication

Winterhoff, Wolfgang, 1953–
OutdoorGuide: West Coast Trail
author/photographer Wolfgang Winterhoff; design Carol Aitken;
editor Aurelia Sedlmair. – 1st ed.

Translation of: Kanada: West Coast Trail
ISBN 0-9734091-2-6

1. Hiking—British Columbia—West Coast Trail—Guidebooks
2. West Coast Trail (B.C.)—Guidebooks
I. Sedlmair, Aurelia, 1966–
II. Title.

GV199.44.C22V35 2006a   917.11'2   C2006-903059-6

Maps © Conrad Stein Verlag
Printed and bound in Canada by Benwell Atkins

Although the author and publisher have take extreme care to ensure that all information in this book is accurate and up to date, they accept no responsibility for any loss, injury or inconvenience sustained by any person using this guide. Readers are responsible to check for changes or updated information with the Pacific Rim National Park authorities and service providers before heading out on the trail.

CONTENTS

FOREWORD 5

SYMBOLS 7

HISTORY OF THE WEST
COAST TRAIL 9
The West Coast Trail Today 11

TRAVEL INFO A–Z 15
Accommodation 15
Boardwalks 15
Cable Cars 16
Equipment 16
First Nations 20
Fishing 21
Food & Drink 22
Backpack Cuisine and
Recipes 22
Trekking and
Expedition Food 25
Water 26
Getting there 26
Stop in Vancouver 27
On to Vancouver Island 29
Stop on Vancouver Island /
Victoria 30
Getting to the Trail 32
Health 36
First Aid Kit 36
Hypothermia 36
Injuries 37
Red Tide 37
Information & Registration
Centres 37
Opening Hours of the
West Coast Trail 38

Juan de Fuca Marine Trail 38
Reservation System 39
Rules of the Trail 42
Safety 42
Tide Tables 46
West Coast Trail for
Everyone 48
Whale Watching 48
Wildlife 49
Wind 54
Chill Factor 54

THE TRAIL IN 7 STAGES
Port Renfrew 59
Index to 7 stages 61
Day 1: Gordon River to
Thrasher Cove 62
Day 2: Thrasher Cove to
Camper Creek 70
Day 3: Camper Creek to
Logan Creek 74
Day 4: Logan Creek to
Cribs Creek 82
Day 5: Cribs Creek to
Tsusiat Falls 91
Day 6: Tsusiat Falls to
Michigan Creek 98
Day 7: Michigan Creek to
Pachena Bay 102
Bamfield 106

EPILOGUE 108

INDEX 110

About the author

Wolfgang Winterhoff came to Canada in 1983 for the first time and fell in love with it. Since then he undertakes canoe and trekking tours mostly in BC and the Yukon. He also organizes tours in Germany for those interested in trekking and canoeing in BC and the Yukon. Sometimes, by special request, he also accompanies them.

The Bowron Lakes Canoe Circuit, the subject of his first guide-book published in Canada, and the West Coast Trail count as his preferred outdoor adventures. After numerous tours on the lakes, he is an expert on the circuit, which is one of the most beautiful canoe routes in the world.

He is considered a competent expert with more than 20 years of experience in Canada's outdoors.

By Wolfgang Winterhoff

THE WEST COAST TRAIL is one of three parts of the Pacific Rim National Park on Vancouver Island that was founded in the mid-sixties. The other two parts are Long Beach with its beautiful sandy beaches and the Broken Island Group in Barkley Sound (the many small islands are an El Dorado for sea-kayakers).

The trail winds through 75 km of temperate rain forest past trees that are often hundreds of years old. Many of these giants have been here since the Vikings landed on Canada's East Coast a thousand years ago.

The almost tropical moist climate and the luscious vegetation are the result of up to 3,000 mm of rain (that is three metres of rain!) annually.

On the West Coast Trail you can still experience a unique, primordial and untamed coastal landscape.

After hiking the trail for the first time in 1994 I have 'done' the trail many times. Despite the challenges, the West Coast Trail is very fascinating to me. On my last tour my fellow hikers and I experienced 6 days of constant rain. The trail took everything out of us but just being in this pure wilderness somehow made it all worthwhile.

If you intend to hike the West Coast Trail keep in mind:

- This hike is not a cakewalk! The continually changing conditions make the trail dangerous and extremely strenuous.
- You have to expect and be prepared for injury; especially the knees and ankles are easily affected.
- When you have insufficient or inadequate clothing, especially during long periods of bad weather (constant rain and fog), you risk hypothermia.
- Some stretches are very challenging and it is difficult to

move forward; be prepared to deal with great physical and psychological strain.

- Give yourself sufficient time. You will likely take longer than expected due to unforeseen circumstances. For example, a few years ago Walbran Creek was so flooded due to heavy rain that crossing the creek was impossible for a number of days and hikers on both sides could not move on.

✋ Inexperienced hikers should not attempt to hike the West Coast Trail! Please be honest with yourself: do you feel fit enough to last through such a trek in the wilderness? If not, schedule the trip for another year – the West Coast Trail will still be there!

☺ Experience has taught me that it is necessary to prepare extremely well for the West Coast Trail and that proper equipment and supplies are mandatory for a successful and enjoyable trip.

☺ The trail changes constantly – the trail itself, the routing, the reservation system, fees, ways of getting there, contact numbers and email addresses etc. – everything is subject to change. Although every effort has been made to provide the most current and accurate information, YOU are responsible for checking and confirming the information to ensure your own safety.

Thanks

First of all, a big 'Thank You' to my reliable comrade-in-arms Kurt Brauneis who has accompanied me on countless trips in recent years. A further heartfelt 'Thank You' to the staff of the Pacific Rim National Park for the vast amount of useful information they have provided which helped me write this guide. I would also like to thank Janine Müller of Windeck-Dattenfeld for looking over the manuscript, Antonius and Rita Kebekus of the outdoor equipment store Kompass in Bad Fredeburg and Mr. Reicher of Simpert Reiter in Augsburg for his excellent advice regarding equipment and supplies.

🖐	ATTENTION
📖	BOOK TIP
🚌	BUS
🚐 ⛺	CAMPSITE (serviced)
⛺	CAMPSITE (tents)
🚗	CAR
🛥	FERRY / BOAT
	FIRST NATIONS RESERVE
🎣	FISHING
ℹ	INFO/REGISTRATION
	LADDER SYSTEM
🛏	LODGE / HOTEL / B&B
	SEAL
☞	SEE UNDER...
☺	TIP
	VIEWPOINT
🐋	WHALE WATCHING

HISTORY OF THE WEST COAST TRAIL

JANUARY 22nd 1906: A STORM is whipping the ocean onto the rugged West Coast of Vancouver Island. The waves are many metres high and thunder against the coast, breaking on the rocks. Within seconds a thick fog rises up hiding everything within it.

The passenger vessel *Valencia* out of San Francisco is heading through the wet inferno to Victoria and Vancouver. The 126 passengers aboard do not suspect that disaster is looming.

The ship runs aground close to the area now called Valencia Bluffs. The heavily damaged vessel stays on the reef for two days before the raging sea literally crushes her. Rescue teams attempt in vain to reach the *Valencia* – all 126 passengers and the crew perish.

Since 1854 more than 60 ships have been shipwrecked on the West Coast of Vancouver Island due to the strong currents and quickly changing weather conditions. In most cases there were no survivors, which is why this region became known as the "Graveyard of the Pacific."

The crew and passengers who were able to reach the apparently safe shore found themselves in an uninhabited and impenetrable wilderness from which there was no escape.

One year after the tragic shipwreck of the *Valencia*, the Canadian government decided to build a lighthouse at Pachena Point as well as a life-saving trail along this infamous coastline. Between 1907 and 1912 sixty men attempted to build a trail using handsaws and horse-drawn equipment. The plan called for a trail, 4 m wide, between Bamfield and Carmanah Point, a distance of 47 km. It was supposed to make it possible for those shipwrecked here to make their way to inhabited areas.

The men intended to follow the existing telegraph lines, which were built in 1890 to connect the lighthouses at Cape Beale and Carmanah Point with other lighthouses and inhabited areas as well as with Victoria.

However, they soon came to realize that it was virtually impossible to carve such a wide trail through the impenetrable wilderness. In the end they only built a 1.5 m wide trail to Carmanah Point.

South of Carmanah Point the shipwreck-survivors had to use the primitive path along the telegraph lines in order to get to safety. Maintenance of the life-saving trail was difficult and expensive. Winter storms continually destroyed the bridges that had been built across steep canyons and constant rain transformed the trail into an impassable swampy bog.

With the development of air rescue and modern navigation the life-saving trail lost its original importance. Maintenance efforts dwindled in the 1940s and were discontinued completely after World War II.

The only part of the trail that was kept in order were 11 kilometers between Bamfield and the Pachena Point lighthouse – everywhere else the wilderness reclaimed the life-saving trail along the "Graveyard of the Pacific."

In the 1960s the Pacific Rim National Park was established on Vancouver Island. With the creation of the new park the life-saving trail once again came to the attention of the public. The Canadian government decided to start maintaining the trail again in 1973.

The trail from Pachena Bay to Carmanah Point (47 km) was completely rebuilt while the 30 kilometers of trail from Carmanah Point to Port Renfrew were simply cleared and straightened. Reconstruction of the trail was completed in 1980.

Some examples of shipwrecks along the West Coast Trail coastline from 1858–1976:

Oyrus	December 1958, by the mouth of Gordon River
St. Clair	November 1948, by Port Renfrew
3-masted barque *Revere*	September 1883 between Thrasher Cove and Owen Point
3-master *William Tell*	December 1865 between Owen Point and Camper Creek

3-master *John Marshall*	November 1860 at mouth of Camper Creek
Barque *Duchess*	November 1887 at mouth of Cullite Creek
Schooner *Wempe Bros.*	October 1901 between Vancouver Point and Bonilla Point
Barque *Lizzie Marshall*	February 1884 between Vancouver Point and Bonilla Point
Schooner *Puritan*	November 1896 between Bonilla Point and Carmanah Point
Schooner *Dane*	December 1890 by Dare Point
Steamship *Santa Rita*	February 1923 at mouth of Cheewhat River
Barque *Skagit*	October 1906 at Clo-oose
Schooner *Raita*	January 1925 at Whyak Point
Schooner *Vesta*	December 1897 between Tsuquadra Point and Tsusiat Point
Barque *Uncle John*	October 1899 at about Tsusiat Point
Steamship *Woodside*	March 1888 at mouth of Trestle Creek
Schooner *Robert Lewers*	April 1923 at mouth of Trestle Creek
Barque *Janet Cowan*	January 1896 between Trestle Creek and Valencia Bluffs
Steamship *Valencia*	January 1906 at Valencia Bluffs
MV *Varsity*	February 1940 at mouth of Billy Goat Creek
Freighter *Uzbekistan*	April 1943 at mouth of Darling River
Steamship *Michigan*	January 1893 at mouth of Michigan Creek
Steamship *Mascotte*	August 1893 at mouth of Michigan Creek
3-master *Becherdass*	July 1879 at mouth of Black River
3-master barque *Sarah*	November 1891 at mouth of Black River
Steamship *Alaskan*	January 1923 by Pachena Bay
Schooner *Soquel*	January 1909 by Pachena Bay

THE WEST COAST TRAIL TODAY

Nowadays the West Coast Trail is a challenge for hikers and trekkers from all over the world. The trail does not appear too daunting with a length of a mere 75 km; however, it is considered one of the most gruelling trails in North America.

Hiking the West Coast Trail requires substantial stamina as well as hiking and camping experience. Beginners are advised NOT to gain their first hiking and trekking experiences on the West Coast Trail – and those suffering from knee or back problems should also reconsider.

In stark contrast to my first experience of the West Coast Trail in 1994 I have noticed on recent trips that attempts have been made to make the hike less tough. Many new boardwalks have been built to keep you out of the mud and make hiking more pleasant. However, please do not misunderstand that last statement! The West Coast Trail remains very challenging.

The boardwalks that wind through the rainforest, sometimes over many kilometers with only a few breaks, make for fairly quick and comfortable walking – provided they are dry. However, if they are wet – which they unfortunately usually are, they are extremely slippery and should be walked very cautiously, otherwise you risk slipping, falling and suffering severe injury.

The boardwalks were primarily built to protect the vegetation but also to keep you out of the mud, at least to some degree.

The annual number of visitors to the West Coast Trail has reached 8,000 in recent years (compared to 'only' 5,200 in 2001). According to Park statistics approximately 70% are foreign hikers. An increase in the number of visitor is impossible unless the Park Administration chooses to change the very strictly supervised reservation system implemented in 1992. The system was designed to protect the magnificent natural environment of this region from the damage that ever increasing numbers of visitors would leave behind. The Park's staff is constantly striving to keep the trail in reasonable condition, which is difficult considering the weather in this region.

Another important reason for the reservation system is that it allows hikers on the trail to feel that they are alone in the wilderness and not on some hopelessly overbooked tourist-excursion.

Hikers planning to go on the West Coast Trail should expect the following:

- A stay of 5–7 days in the wilderness.
- A trail that is often extremely challenging. You should plan a minimum of 2 days for the 22 km stretch between Gordon River and Walbran Creek.
- Slippery boardwalks, a muddy trail and a rocky and rugged coastline.
- Cable cars, crossing rivers and creeks and climbing up and down very steep and tall ladders.
- Bridges and ladders that have been destroyed by storms.
- Moderate coastal rain forest with the corresponding climate. Precipitation of about 3,000 mm annually is normal in this region. The weather can change in an instant.
- Accidents and injury. It may take more than 24 hours before help arrives.

ACCOMMODATION

There are countless choices for accommodation on the way to and from the West Coast Trail – too many and too varied to list them all in this guide. Whenever I head out to hike the trail, I have a number of Bed & Breakfasts or hotels I like to stay in. I happily provide their contact information, however, you will find more complete listings, with detailed information on location, availability and prices as well as booking details on the following websites:

www.oceansidetourism.com
www.zapbc.com
www.bcadventure.com
www.vancouverisland.com
www.islands.bc.ca
www.wcbbia.com

BOARDWALKS

The boardwalks were built by the Park Administration and measure many kilometers. They were constructed to protect the vegetation (8,000 hikers annually will leave their mark, whether they are careful or not) and to provide hikers with a more comfortable hike.

However, be careful. These walkways are tricky! They are usually very slippery due to the moisture and many of them have started to rot. It is very easy to loose your footing, to break through or to otherwise hurt yourself when your feet slide out from under you.

On one of my first hikes on the West Coast Trail I had my own, very painful, experience. I slipped in such an unfortunate manner that I pulled a muscle in my thigh and was in severe pain for the next few days on the trail.

CABLE CARS

The cable car is a basic wooden or metal box that is just large enough to hold one person and a backpack. This box hangs on a wire and moves forward when the passenger pulls on a wire or rope that is run through a pulley system. There are 5 cable cars on the trail located at Camper, Cullite and Carmanah Creeks as well as at Klanawa and Darling Rivers.

They are all very safe, although not for the faint of heart – but still better than wet feet. Sometimes falling trees damage the cable cars and make them unusable. In this case, you have no other choice but to wade through the creek or river. If wading across to the other side is impossible, the Park Administration usually provides a ferry service.

These ferries sometimes run only at a specific time, therefore you have to keep these crossing times in mind when working out your time schedule.

EQUIPMENT

Outdoor enthusiasts love to talk about equipment and authors of outdoor guidebooks like to write even more than is already being said about it. I am not excluding myself here, especially when it comes to the West Coast Trail. For those who choose to hike the West Coast Trail the best is barely good enough! That is not an exaggeration but is based on years of personal experience. All hikers with West Coast Trail experience will definitely agree with me on that.

When I mentioned to a park warden I met on my most recent hike on the West Coast Trail that I was writing this guide, he asked me to tell people to leave their jeans and cotton T-shirts at home. They are just not appropriate clothing for the West Coast Trail!

The reason should be obvious: wet cotton clothing (including jeans) does not dry very well. On the West Coast Trail dampness is a fact of life. If constant rain or high humidity do not succeed, then your sweat from physical exertion certainly will leave you at least damp if not soaked. You risk hypothermia (☞ *Hypothermia*) if you stay in your wet clothes too long. Hypothermia is one of the reasons hikers have to be evacuated in order to save their lives. (More on this later.)

Even if you change your clothes frequently, your wet things will take a long time to dry (if they dry at all!), and no one carries enough clothing to be able to change at least once a day.

Materials that wick sweat away from the body and dry quickly definitely have the advantage. These materials are usually made of polyester or a polyester-mix fabric (65 % polyester, 35 % cotton) for pants as well as fleece shirt or sweaters.

These materials have one added benefit: they are very light-weight. Weight is as important as quality when on the trail. A backpack that is too heavy will definitely have a negative impact on your experience. I vividly remember my first trip – the extra weight of my backpack made it sheer torture.

Rain jacket and rain pants are a must and I recommend you choose items that are made of a waterproof yet at the same time breathable material that dries quickly. (Be aware though that the ideal waterproof jacket or pants in which you will not sweat when you exert yourself has not yet been invented.)

Materials such as Gore-Tex, Texapore or Sympatex work well but you will still sweat in them and not all the moisture will be drawn out.

The same holds true for shoes. If you choose to save money on your footwear, you are taking a foolish risk with your feet and your health. Running shoes are definitely inappropriate on the trail. My friends and I were speechless when, just before the end of our trip, we encountered a couple, just heading out, wearing light runners as well as carrying otherwise inadequate equipment. I could not help myself; I had to warn them, for their own safety. However, they chose to ignore my words, gave me a patronizing smile and continued on their way.

About two thirds of the West Coast Trail winds through thick rainforest while one third runs along the beach. In the forest the trail is a mix of slippery boardwalks, thick entwined roots, knee-deep mud and water puddles as well as tree trunks. You have to be extremely aware of the dangers and take care that you do not injure yourself, especially with improper footwear.

Although the path along the beach promises more comfortable walking, there are also many rocky stretches to conquer and you feet and ankles will thank you for wearing appropriate hiking boots with sufficient support.

Except for shoes and socks my equipment is almost exclusively from Jack Wolfskin. They use excellent materials and produce clothes and equipment that is durable and functional at an affordable price.

The following is my personal basic equipment list from my last trip on the West Coast Trail, which can serve as a guideline for yours. Of course everyone has their own idea what equipment and clothing to pack, but some things are important and just plain necessary and should not be forgotten.

Camping Equipment

- Backpack, 65 liters, with rain covering
- Tent for 2 with necessary accessories
- Tent repair kit
- Self-inflatable sleeping mat
- Sleeping bag (artificial fibre filling)
- Trangia gas burner
- 2 liters gas
- Lightweight pot or pan
- Cup, plate, cutlery

Clothing

- Weatherproof jacket
- Rain jacket and pants
- Hiking boots with a set of spare bootlaces

- 2 pairs hiking socks
- Gaiters
- 2 sets functional underwear (draws away moisture)
- Fleece sweater or jacket
- 2 pairs hiking pants (quick-drying)
- Sandals or running shoes (to wear around camp)
- Toque or hat/cap

Accessories

- Binoculars
- Camera and film
- Sewing kit
- Knife
- Matches/lighter and a candle
- 2 lightweight water/drinking bottles
- Head- or flashlight
- 20 m light rope
- Water treatment tablets/drops

All in all that adds up to approximately 23 kg of equipment and supplies. In case you need to add anything to your equipment or supplies, you can do so easily in Seattle, Vancouver or Victoria.

3 Vets
2200 Yukon Street, Vancouver, BC
Tel: 604-872 5475

Coast Mountain Sports
2201 West 4th Avenue, Vancouver, BC
Tel: 604-731 6181

Mountain Equipment Coop (MEC)
130 W. Broadway, Vancouver, BC
Tel: 604-872 7858
Web: www.mec.ca

Pacific Trekking
1305 Government St, Victoria, BC
Tel: 250-388 7088 or 1 800-565 1399
Web: www.pacifictrekking.com

REI
222 Yale Ave N, Seattle, WA 98109
Tel: 206-223 1944, or 888-873 1938
Web: www.rei.com

Robinson's Outdoor Store
1307 Broad Street, Victoria, BC
Tel: 250-385 3429
Web: www.robinsonsoutdoors.com

Canadian Tire Stores in many locations throughout Canada often offer decent equipment in their outdoor department:
www.canadiantire.ca

FIRST NATIONS

For some years the Ditidaht, Huu-ay-aht and Pacheedaht First Nations who live along the West Coast Trail have been offering their services to visitors to the area and to hikers of the trail. They have succeeded in sharing their culture and traditions with the West Coast Trail hikers who are walking on historic terrain on the lifesaving-trail at the "Graveyard of the Pacific." Their ideas and commitment have contributed much to the hikers experience.

Thousands of hikers visit the West Coast Trail every year and experience its magnificent natural wonders. However, in my opinion, you can only really experience the West Coast Trail, if you also get a glimpse of the life and history of the First Nations that live there. Their history is also a part of the trail's history.

You can find information regarding annual events and activities offered by these First Nations as follows:

Ditidaht First Nations
Port Alberni, BC
Tel: 250-745 3333 or 250-745 3310, Fax: 250-745 3332

Huu-Ay-Aht First Nations
Bamfield, BC
Tel: 250-745 3080, Fax: 250-728 3081
Web: www.huuayaht.ca

Pacheedaht First Nations
Port Renfrew, BC
Tel: 250-647 5521, Fax: 250-647 5561

The Quu'as West Coast Trail Society is a partnership between the First Nations and Parks Canada that is designed to maintain the cultural and traditional history of the West Coast Trail.

Quu'as West Coast Trail Office
Tel: 250-723 4393, Web: www.alberni.net/quuas

The First Nations people living along the West Coast Trail are proud that people from all over the world come to experience the beauty and splendour of their land. Still, hikers must respect the private property of the First Nations. Your West Coast Trail experience will be greatly enriched if you try to see your surroundings through the eyes of the native people and honour their commitment to preserving their lands.

FISHING

Fishing is permitted on the West Coast Trail but you have to carry the appropriate licenses (Non-Tidal Angling License and Tidal Waters Sports Fishing License) and follow the regulations and closures. You can find more detailed information in the annual fishing guide, available free of charge in the sporting good stores that sell the necessary licenses. The Information and Registration Centres do not sell fishing licenses.

FOOD AND DRINK

Besides good equipment and clothing, food is the most important component to consider when planning your hike. The type of food you choose may decide whether the hike is fun despite the strain and effort required or becomes torture.

On all my hikes on the West Coast Trail I take care to choose food that provides a lot of energy, is lightweight and quickly prepared. The last point seems especially important to me since there is nothing worse than having to fiddle for a long time to prepare a meal in extremely bad weather or when you are completely exhausted.

Backpack Cuisine and Recipes

As a guideline I have provided the list of food items I took with me on my last 7-day hike on the West Coast Trail:

- 1.5 kg granola per person
- 1 can pumpernickel bread per person
- Peanut butter, jam
- Hard cheese
- Bacon bits (prepared before you head out)
- Margarine/butter
- Honey
- Assorted spices (packed in re-sealable plastic bags)
- Pre-mixed dry dough ingredients
- Assorted trekking meals: pasta with cheese sauce, vegetarian risotto, pea soup, potato-vegetable stew with tofu, pasta with pesto sauce, chicken curry with rice, pasta with tomato sauce
- For those in-between snacks: beef jerky, 2 power/energy bars per person per day, trail-mix, dried fruit
- Coffee, tea, cocoa, energy drink

☺ Every hiker on the West Coast Trail should drink enough: 3–4 liters are advisable because you loose a lot of water through perspiration. Your water bottle should always be full. You can refill it at the countless small creeks and rivers along the way (☞ *Water*). This granola mix is quite easy to make and I take it with me on every trip into the wilderness:

ARLENE'S CRISPY TRAIL GRANOLA
> 1000 g rolled oats
> 200 g shredded coconut
> 200 g sunflower seeds
> 150 g sliced almonds
> 100 g oatmeal
> 100 g wheat germ
> 500 g ground mixed nuts
> *Mix everything well in a bowl*
> 500 g honey (1 glass, warmed in the microwave or hot water bath)
> *Add after baking (otherwise it hardens!):*
> 150 g soy nuts
> 200 g raisins

Mix the liquid honey with the contents in the bowl, then spread the mixture evenly over two baking sheets, covering the bottom of the sheets. Pre-heat the oven to 180°C, and bake the mixture for 5–8 minutes. When the edges of the mixture on the baking sheet start to brown, stir, then continue baking for another 5–8 minutes. Continue this process until the entire mixture is slightly browned.

This crunchy granola is very nutritious and also very tasty. It keeps well in a tin cookie can after cooling off. Before my tours, I add powdered milk and pack the granola in re-sealable plastic bags.

BANNOCK
If you do not want to take pumpernickel or other bread with you, you can try baking the bread of the North American trappers

yourself. You can try it in a pan (careful, not too much heat) or on flat rocks that you have heated in the fire, as in the photo below.

INGREDIENTS

    4 cups whole-wheat flour
    2 tablespoons powdered egg
    2 tablespoons powdered milk
    2 teaspoons dried yeast or baking powder
    1 pinch each of sugar and salt

Mix everything well and pack in a re-sealable plastic bag. When you want to bake the bannock, knead in enough margarine and water to make firm dough, then form a flat cake. If you like, you can also add bacon bits and onion or garlic flakes etc.

☺ A special treat for breakfast: warm bannock with peanut butter and jam.

BACON PANCAKES

    2 cups flour
    1.5 cups powdered milk
    1 teaspoon salt
    3 tablespoons powdered egg

Mix well and package in re-sealable plastic bags. When ready to make pancakes, add bacon bits and enough water to make fairly liquid dough. Bake pancakes in the pan.

AUSTRIAN KAISERSCHMARRN
- 2 cups flour
- 2 tablespoons powdered egg
- 2 tablespoons powdered milk
- 1 heaping teaspoon potato starch
- 1 pinch of salt
- Raisins as desired

Mix well and package in re-sealable plastic bags. When ready to make the 'Emperors Pancake,' add enough water to make fairly liquid dough, add a bit of margarine and fry in the pan while stirring and breaking up the pancake. Before serving, sprinkle with a little sugar or honey.

> *Basic Essentials Cooking in the Outdoors*, 2nd, Cliff Jacobson, ISBN 0762704268, Globe Pequot, 1999

Trekking and Expedition Food

The advantages of 'bagged' food, freeze dried meals, are obvious. This type of food has the reputation of being expensive and not exactly pleasing to the palate – however, that is a misconception. In actuality these meal can be purchased for an acceptable price and because they are lightweight, they are easy to take along. As to the taste, well, the smart outdoor enthusiast should have sufficient imagination to pep up meals by adding onions, garlic or a few spices.

Freeze-dried food is also an excellent source of energy. When the body has to work hard over long periods of time, it is important to supply it with sufficient protein, fat, carbohydrates, vitamins and minerals. Furthermore, the meals are usually made without preservatives, keep for years (if need be), are safely packaged and take up little space. Most outdoor equipment stores sell them.

🖐 Caution! If you are entering Canada from the USA or another foreign country, please remember that no meat or meat-products may be imported into Canada due to BSE. This includes meat in trekking food pouches.

If you intend to bring freeze-dried food with you into Canada, make sure that they are vegetarian meals only. You can find accurate information regarding the Canadian Food Inspection Agency regulations on the Internet at:
    www.inspection.gc.ca

Water

Stomach problems are primarily caused by unclean or contaminated drinking water. You are well advised to always filter your water or to use water tablets/drops to make it safe. You can find water tablets or purification drops at your local outdoor equipment store.

☺ I recommend that you additionally enrich your drinking water with magnesium and/or calcium tablets in order to maintain the necessary levels of these minerals in your body.

GETTING THERE

Depending on your point of origin, you may arrive in Vancouver, Victoria or Nanaimo by bus, train, plane or automobile. Your travel agent will probably be able to assist with the necessary arrangements. The following provides information on how to proceed from there.

If you are travelling to Canada from Europe as a citizen of a European country, you require a passport that is at least valid for the entire duration of your stay, preferably longer (6 months is recommended). If you are coming from the USA (born there /naturalized citizen/permanent US resident), you have to provide proof of citizenship (passport or an original or certified birth certificate) plus picture ID or your passport together with your Green Card. It is your responsibility to have the proper documents! Check exact requirements at:

www.bctravel.com/travel2.html

Stop in Vancouver

On the shore of the Pacific Ocean, framed by the majestic Coast Mountains, Vancouver is considered a pearl on the Pacific and one of the most beautiful cities in the world. When you arrive at Vancouver International Airport your first impression will be of a lot of glass, rocks, a waterfall and many sculptures by renowned West Coast First Nation artists that govern the architecture of the airport and introduce you to a modern and vibrant city.

Canada's most westerly metropolis has a population of over 2 million. The public transit system is reasonable and efficient, providing visitors with the opportunity to get to most remote spots. The many and varied cultural offerings, beautiful parks and beaches, excellent restaurants as well as great accommodation invite to stay a while.

Depending on your arrival time in Vancouver, you may want to stay overnight to enjoy the sights and amenities of the city before you continue on to Vancouver Island and the West Coast Trail. For details check out:

www.tourismvancouver.com

☺ If you so choose, you can be in the middle of the wilderness within 30 minutes from the city centre. However, you should not miss Stanley Park, Granville Island, Gastown or Grouse Mountain while you are here.

🛏 OVERNIGHT

There are many different types of accommodation available in

WEST COAST TRAIL

Vancouver. My favourites are listed below but if you would like more choice, check the following website:

www.hellobc.com

The Abercorn Inn is very close to Vancouver International Airport and offers a free bus transfer from and to the airport. The hotel is part of the Best Western chain and is quite reasonable.

The Abercorn Inn
9260 Bridgeport Road, Richmond, BC
Tel: 604-270 7576, Fax: 604-270 0001

Poole's Bed & Breakfast in North Vancouver, about 20 minutes from downtown, is a small, family atmosphere B&B run by Doreen and Arthur Poole. The rooms are comfortable and the breakfast, included in the price for the night, is sumptuous. That makes this B&B an easy recommendation, especially if you would like to spend a few days sightseeing in Vancouver before or after your West Coast Trail experience.

Poole's Bed & Breakfast
421 West St. James Road, North Vancouver, BC
Tel: 604-987 4594, Fax: 604-987 4283
Email: rapoole@lightspeed.ca

☺ Before I get into the various ways you can continue on to the West Coast Trail, one more tip: You probably want to hike the West Coast Trail together with someone else. If you are not travelling to Vancouver, Victoria or Nanaimo by car, it is advisable to rent one at the airport or in one of those cities, even if the car stays unused at the southern or northern trailhead for 6–8 days while you are off hiking. Renting a car is not that expensive, it will make you more flexible and save time.

For example, the cost of transport for 3 people from Vancouver to the southern or northern trailhead and back is almost as much

28

as renting a car for a week. If you can, reserve ahead as rental companies tend to be quite booked in the summer months.

On to Vancouver Island

 BY BUS

Pacific Coach Lines runs every 2 hours between Vancouver International Airport and the Victoria Bus Depot. Travel time is approximately 3.5 hours including the ferry ride. It is usually not necessary to make a reservation and tickets can be purchased prior to departure at the bus. If you are in downtown Vancouver, the bus also departs from the Bus Terminal as well as the Cruise Ship Terminal.

> **Pacific Coach Lines**
> 1150 Station Street, Vancouver, BC
> Tel: 604-662 8074
> Web: www.pacificcoach.com

 BY FERRY

Depending on the route you want to travel, BC Ferries usually run between the mainland and the island at least every 2 hours. In the summer, on weekends and holidays reservations are very highly recommended, otherwise you may have to wait at least one if not more sailings.

If you want to hike the trail from north to south, you should take the ferry from Vancouver/Tsawwassen to Nanaimo/Duke Point or from Vancouver/Horseshoe Bay to Nanaimo/Departure Bay; travel time on the ferry is generally 1 hour 40 minutes.

Should you prefer to hike the trail from south to north, take the ferry from Vancouver/Tsawwassen to Victoria/Swartz Bay; travel time is approximately 1 hour 35 minutes.

> **BC Ferries**
> Tel: 1-888-BC FERRY (1-888-223 3779) from anywhere in N. America
> Web: www.bcferries.com

The Victoria Clipper, a sleek, high-speed catamaran passenger ferry, travels a number of times daily between Seattle and Victoria. For directions, schedules, fares and reservations contact them at:

Victoria Clipper
2701 Alaskan Way, Pier 69, Seattle, WA 98121
Tel: 206-448 5000, Toll free: 800-888 2535
Web: www.victoriaclipper.com

There are also two ferry services from Port Angeles into Victoria: the Victoria Express, which operates seasonally, and Black Ball Transport, which runs the MV *Coho*, a vehicle and passenger ferry, all year round.

Black Ball Transport Inc.
East Railroad Ave, Port Angeles, WA, 98362
Tel: 360-457 4491, Fax: 360-457 4493
Web: www.cohoferry.com

Victoria Express
Tel: 360-452 8088
Email: info@victoriaexpress.com
Web: www.victoriaexpress.com

Stop on Vancouver Island/Victoria

Victoria, incorporated in 1862 and capital city of the Province of British Columbia since 1871, is worth a trip. The city of flowers and parks is located at the southern tip of Vancouver Island and boasts the mildest climate in Canada. The city has more than 60 public parks and is immeasurably enhanced by many Victorian heritage buildings. In the Inner Harbour the world famous Empress Hotel and the Legislature of the Province of British Columbia offer an impressive view. As a special treat you may enjoy Afternoon Tea in the lobby of the Empress Hotel, reservations are recommended in high season and proper attire is required – no jeans allowed.

🐋 Another highlight you may not want to miss in Victoria is whale watching. (☞ *Whale Watching*) The Strait of Juan de Fuca provides excellent conditions for viewing whales and many companies in the Inner Harbour offer these tours. The boats and their operators have to follow strict guidelines when they encounter whales and other marine animals for the protection of both, animals and passengers. There are a number of reputable companies that offer these tours. My best experience was with Springtide Charters, a founding member of Whale Watch Operator's Association Northwest.

Springtide Charters
1207 Wharf Street, Victoria, BC
Toll free: 1-800-470-3474
Web: www.springtidecharters.com

ℹ️ For more information on the sights as well as accommodation, check out:
    www.victoriatourism.com

🛏️ OVERNIGHT

Joan Brown's Bed & Breakfast
729 Pemberton Road, Victoria, BC
Tel: 604-592 5929 (about 5 minutes from Victoria's city centre)

Gus's In Town Bed & Breakfast
430 Government Street, Victoria, BC
Tel: 250-383 7938

🛏️ OVERNIGHT IN QUALICUM BEACH
The Blue Willow Bed & Breakfast owned by Maxine Morris is located in Qualicum Beach, about 40 km north of Nanaimo. It is a beautiful B&B with an excellent breakfast in charming surroundings. It is possible to leave any luggage not needed on the trail

here until you return. Qualicum Beach is well suited as a base from which to explore many of Vancouver Island's sights.

You can organize a transfer from the B&B to Port Alberni in order to take the West Coast Trail Express to the trailhead. If you are arriving in Nanaimo by ferry and plan to stay at this B&B, you can take the bus from the Nanaimo Bus Depot to Qualicum Beach.

Blue Willow Bed & Breakfast, Maxine Morris
524 Quatna Road, Qualicum Beach, BC, V9K 1B4
Tel: 250-752 9052, Fax: 250-752 9031
Email: bwillow@island.net
Web: www.bluewillowguesthouse.ca

Getting to the Trail

 BY BUS

Reservations on the West Coast Trail Express are definitely recommended. Schedules are available online, at the Information Centres at the respective trailheads as well as from the bus drivers, although it is worthwhile to make arrangements prior to arrival at the various pick-up/drop off points. The routes are:

- Victoria – Gordon River – Port Renfrew
- Victoria – Pachena Bay – Bamfield
- Nanaimo – Pachena Bay – Bamfield
- Gordon River and Port Renfrew – Nitinat – Pachena Bay – Bamfield
- Port Alberni – Pachena Bay – Bamfield
- Bamfield – Nitinat – Gordon River – Port Renfrew
- Pachena Bay – Nitinat – Gordon River – Port Renfrew
- Pachena Bay – Port Alberni – Nanaimo – Victoria
- Gordon River and Port Renfrew – Victoria

If you choose to hike the trail from north to south you can take the West Coast Trail Express from Nanaimo/Departure Bay via Port Alberni and Bamfield to reach the northern trailhead at Pachena Bay. Travel time is approximately 3 hours.

If you prefer to hike the trail from south to north, you should take the West Coast Trail Express from the bus depot in Victoria to Port Renfrew/Gordon River, the southern trailhead. Travel time is approximately 2.5 hours.

West Coast Trail Express
Tel: 250-477 8700, Fax: 250-477 8774
Toll free in Canada: 1-888 999 2288
Email: bus@trailbus.com, Web: www.trailbus.com

 BY BOAT

Hikers planning to do the West Coast Trail from north to south have another attractive option: take the West Coast Trail Express to Port Alberni, then continue on the heritage vessel MV *Lady Rose* or the MV *Frances Barkley*. These two ships are combined freight and passenger vessels that have been travelling daily between Port Alberni, Ucluelet and Bamfield for the last sixty years. Their run takes them from Port Alberni through Albert Inlet to the Broken Island Group and back.

Departure from Port Alberni is at 8 AM, arrival in Bamfield at about 12:30 PM, depending on the freight and cargo or mail deliveries to be made. It is definitely advisable to make reservations.

In order to reach the northern trailhead at Pachena Bay you can either catch the West Coast Trail Express or walk the remaining 5 km. If you have finished your hike at Pachena Bay, one of the two ships can take you from Bamfield back to Port Alberni.

Alberni (Lady Rose) Marine Services
Tel: 250-723 8313, Fax: 250-723 8314, Toll-free (between April 1 to September 30): 800-663 7192
Web: www.ladyrosemarine.com

Juan de Fuca Water Taxi (Service between Port Renfrew, Nitinat Narrows and Bamfield)
Tel: 250-755 6578

Butch Jack Ferry Service
(Service to and from Gordon River trailhead)
Tel: 250-647 5517, Fax: 250-647 0044

🚐 BY CAR

If you are taking a car to Bamfield or Pachena Bay, the starting point for the hike from north to south, follow the signs from Port Alberni. It will take you approximately 2 hours to drive the 90 km gravel road.

✋ This road is a bit dangerous because logging trucks travel on the same road, at least on working days. The drivers generally keep to the middle of the road, drive fast and seem to dislike braking.

If you meet up with one of these trucks in dry weather, you will be enveloped in a huge dust cloud with zero visibility. For safety reasons you should drive to the side of the road, stop and let the dust settle. Rocks that are catapulted against your car and windshield are an added danger.

When it rains the road becomes very slippery so drive with caution.

From Victoria it will take you approximately 2.5 hours to reach the southern trailhead at Port Renfrew/Gordon River.

You can park you car at either trailhead, therefore this is not really a factor in deciding which way to hike the trail.

✋ Do NOT leave any valuables in your car!

☺ On our last trip on the West Coast Trail we parked our car at the northern trailhead and then took the bus to the southern trailhead at Port Renfrew where we started our hike the next day. This way we had our own car at the end of the hike, which was very convenient.

☺ If you choose not to hike the entire trail, you have the option of hiking only a portion of it (☞ *West Coast Trail for Everyone*).

Travel to Bamfield/Port Renfrew as described, then hike from the Pachena Bay trailhead to Nitinat Narrows, which is approximately half of the total distance. This part appears to be more attractive than the stretch between Gordon River and Nitinat Narrows.

From Nitinat Narrows you can take the Nitinat Lake Water taxi to Nitinat Village and then continue on the West Coast Trail Express to Bamfield.

✋ The Nitinat Water taxi runs only once a day between Nitinat Narrows and Nitinat Village, usually at 5 PM. You therefore have to arrive there on time, otherwise you have to stay on the campground there and lose almost an entire day.

✋ The West Coast Trail Express only makes a run to Nitinat Village if there are passengers, which means you must make a reservation for travel back to Bamfield from there.

✋ It is not permitted to start the West Coast Trail hike at Nitinat Village or rather at the Nitinat Narrows. Nitinat Narrows is solely an EXIT point. The trailheads at Gordon River and Pachena Bay are the ONLY possible starting points.

HEALTH

First Aid Kit

Rescue/emergency blanket
Antibiotics
Painkillers
Flu & cold medicine
Muscle cream
Sunscreen
Cream for light burns
Insect repellent
Calamine lotion
Japanese healing balm/Tiger balm
Band Aids
Disinfectant spray
Second skin spray/stick
Bandages
2 elastic bandages
1 triangular sling
Bodyglide (for prevention of jock itch)

Hypothermia

Hypothermia means "suffering from exposure." The body temperature falls below 35 degrees Celsius. First signs of hypothermia include shivering, general aching, high blood pressure (over 150/100), racing pulse (over 100) and pale, cold and clammy skin followed by impaired thinking and decision-making.

What to do: do not sleep. Instead move around a lot and slowly warm up the body. The heat should come from the outside, i.e. an emergency blanket, warm steam or through another person's body heat. The room or tent temperature should be raised if possible.

🖐 If your body temperature falls below 30 degrees Celsius it is life-threatening as it causes irregular heartbeat (cardiac arrhythmia). Immediate medical attention is required!

During long periods of bad weather you run the risk of hypothermia due to inadequate equipment or improper clothing.

Injuries

You can easily get injured on the West Coast Trail. Before you know it, you have slipped on the slimy boardwalk or stumbled over some entwined roots. Usually the resulting injuries are minor sprains, strained tendons or bruises and small cuts. You should carry the proper creams and bandages in your kit. Sometimes creams and lotions unfortunately do not have the desired effect. Below are a few hints and tips given to me by experts and a few that are based on my own experience:

- A cream containing Heparin helps to soothe minor bruises. Massaging the cream in lightly helps the clotted blood to spread and reduces the pain.
- The same cream is effective on sprains and pulled muscles or tendons.
- Before applying the cream, you should quickly cool the bruise using an ice spray. Do not passively stretch the injured body part.
- Muscle cramps are soothed by stretching the affected muscles, slowly warming up the injured area and especially through the intake of minerals like magnesium and calcium.

Red Tide

Only double-chambered molluscs like mussels, clams and oysters are affected by red tide. Do not eat them, as the chance of being poisoned is great. You can get accurate, current information regarding red tide and where to you have to beware at the Registration and Information Centres at the respective trailheads.

INFORMATION & REGISTRATION CENTRES

Hikers receive detailed and current information about the trail as well as a trail package from the staff at the Registration and

Information Centres. It is mandatory to register here to receive the Trail Pass. Before you head out, you will also be shown a video about the trail during the orientation session.

The Registration and Information Centre of the northern trailhead is located in Pachena Bay, a beautiful bay about 5 km out of Bamfield. Camping is permitted at Pachena Bay.

May 1 – September 30, Hours: 9 AM – 5 PM
Tel/Fax: 250-728 3234

The Registration and Information Centre for the southern trailhead is located in Port Renfrew, at the mouth of the Gordon River. There is a lovely campground here.

May 1 – September 30, Hours: 9 AM – 5 PM
Tel: 250-647 5434, Fax: 250-647 0016

OPENING HOURS OF THE WEST COAST TRAIL

The West Coast Trail is open from May 1 – September 30 every year. Outside of these months the trail is closed to any hikers and visitors. Hiking the trail out of season would be very dangerous. The short winter days leave only a short time period for hiking safely and in case of accident or injury rescue might take days.

Long periods of rain make the trail impassable and the sea, churned up by severe winter storms, rages over the beaches so that no resting place may be found. Camping in the woods would be too dangerous since strong winds often uproot trees and blow down branches. Furthermore, there is no ferry service between Port Renfrew and the Gordon River trailhead or to Nitinat Narrows.

JUAN DE FUCA MARINE TRAIL

The Juan de Fuca Marine Trail leads from Botanical Beach close to Port Renfrew along the rough and spectacular coastline of

Vancouver Island to China Beach. It is 47 km long. The trail was established in 1994 for the Commonwealth Games that took place in
Victoria that year and is not connected with the West Coast Trail.

The Juan de Fuca Marine Trail offers spectacular coastal scenery
and some rainforest but cannot be compared with the adventure
and experience of the West Coast Trail.

As a wilderness trail it should only be hiked with appropriate
equipment and clothing but it is far less challenging than the
West Coast Trail. It is a good alternative for hikers who are wary of
attempting the West Coast Trail.

You should plan 3–4 days to hike the entire trail but it is also
possible to simply do day trips to experience the magnificent
coast. There are four trailheads that provide access to the trail. At
each of them you will find a Park Information Centre and a picnic
spot. Reservations are not necessary nor do you have to pay a registration or visitor fee for using the Juan de Fuca Marine Trail.

Juan de Fuca Marine Trail Information
Tel: 250-391 2300, Fax: 250-478 9211
Web: www.gov.bc.ca/bcparks

RESERVATION SYSTEM

In the late 1980s and in the early 1990s the number of visitors to
the West Coast Trail increased steadily and in 1992 the administration of the Pacific Rim National Park felt it necessary to imple-
ment a quota and reservation system. The system was modified
in 1994. Since then 52 hikers are allowed onto the West Coast Trail
per day when it is open; 26 hikers from the southern trailhead at
Port Renfrew/Gordon River and another 26 from the northern
trailhead at Bamfield/Pachena Bay. The total number of hikers in
one season totals just under 8,000. Twenty of these hikers at each
trailhead are on the reservation list, the remaining six respectively
are from the waiting list. The spaces from the waiting list are al-
located on a first-come-first-served basis.

For a fee every hiker can purchase a detailed route map (1:50.000) at the Information and Registration Centres. This map is regularly updated (every few years) and depicts the exact route including measurements in kilometers and also contains a lot of helpful information for the trip.

Maintenance of the West Coast Trail costs the BC Ministry of Parks at least $ 750,000.00 annually. Therefore, when the quota and reservation system was established, a user fee payable by every hiker on the West Coast Trail was also implemented.

Note: A reservation can only be made within a time period of 3 months. For example, as of March 1 you can reserve a starting time within the month of May, as of April 1 for a starting time within the months of May and June, as of May 1 for a starting time within the months of May, June and July etc.

Before you place the call, you should have your credit card ready as well as the following information:
- Home address
- Number of persons (Groups may have a maximum of 10 persons, except for school groups hiking the trail between May 1–20 and September 20–24, these groups may have up to 18 persons.)
- Desired starting date as well as two alternative starting dates
- Desired starting point – either the trailhead at Port Renfrew/ Gordon River or at Bamfield/Pachena Bay

Other information to keep in mind:
- At the time you make your reservation, a non-refundable reservation fee of $ 25.00 will be charged to your credit card. This includes the reservation fee, an information package that contains the West Coast Trail Preparation Guide as well as the official, waterproof route map of the West Coast Trail. You may also download the preparation guide from: http://sookenet.com/activity/trails/wctguide.html

- A change fee of $6.42 will be charged if you choose to change your starting date later on.
- Should you arrive at one of the trailheads without a reservation you may receive one of the six waiting list-spots (which are given out at each trailhead respectively). Any reserved places that are not claimed by 3 PM on the day you are to start your hike will be added to the waiting list.
- Do not plan to do the hike without a reservation, hoping to receive one of the spots on the waiting list because this may mean waiting for 1–3 days, especially from July to mid-September.

✋ If you have a reservation, you should register by 3:30 PM on the day before your starting date. Should you arrive later, i.e. on your starting day, you must register by 3 PM or your space will be given to someone on the waiting list.

FEES PER PERSON FOR HIKING THE WEST COAST TRAIL

Payable at time of reservation/change:	
Reservation fee	$25.00
Change of Reservation fee	$6.42
Payable at Registration & Information Centre:	
West Coast Trail User fee	$90.00
Gordon River Ferry	$14.00
Nitinat Narrows Ferry	$14.00

Changes to the fee structure are always possible. Please confirm at: www.pc.gc.ca/pn-np/bc/pacificrim/visit/tarifs_fees_E.asp?Park=21
    Anyone who stays overnight on the West Coast Trail, even those who only want to hike part of the trail, has to pay these fees.

✋ In order to use the ferries, you have to present the official West Coast Trail Pass that every hiker receives at the start from the staff at the Registration Centre after completing the registration procedure. If you do not have a pass, you are not entitled to ferry service.

RULES OF THE TRAIL

- Every visitor should contribute his or her share to maintain the pristine and unique coastal wilderness of the West Coast Trail.

- It is forbidden to collect plants, rocks or shells while on the West Coast Trail, as the trail is located in the Pacific Rim National Park.

- Anything you bring in must be taken back out! Leave only footprints, take nothing but pictures.

- Campfires are only permitted on the beach and must be kept as small as possible.

- The West Coast Trail passes through a number of Native reserves. That land is private property and should be respected as such by every visitor!

SAFETY

Every visitor to the West Coast Trail is required to register with the staff at one of the Registration and Information Centres before starting the hike. This enables the Park Authorities to monitor the number of hikers on the trail at any given time.

Any necessary rescue or evacuation measures can be executed much more precisely. As long as the trail is open to the public, park wardens patrol the West Coast Trail by boat or on foot in case help is required. They evacuate the injured by boat or helicopter and transport them to the next hospital or First Aid Station. If rescue or evacuation is unavoidable, be prepared for additional costs for transport and accommodation.

If you are injured shortly after starting your hike, you should definitely NOT continue. A swollen knee will certainly not improve when carrying a heavy backpack. Under such circumstances you would be wise to turn back.

Every year a number of accidents make rescues and evacuations of injured hikers imperative. This represents a considerable effort and expenditure, not only of a financial nature. In the past, these rescues and evacuations were necessary:

1996	29
1997	44
1998	86
1999	49
2000	102
2001	82
2002	78
2003	92
2004	124

According to information from the park administration, most of these evacuations were the result of hikers taking foolish risks, being over-confident and not sufficiently prepared. However, sometimes there are also other reasons for evacuation measures. A few years ago hikers had to be flown out by helicopter due to a mud slide on the trail.

We experienced one example of how not to do it in the early summer of 2001: a group of 8 people, including one woman, started their hike around lunchtime from the southern trailhead at Gordon River. After crossing on the ferry, the woman stumbled when she climbed out of the boat and fell, hitting her head on a rock. After a little while she thought she was okay and the group continued on their hike.

That evening in Thrasher Cove, the first camping opportunity on the West Coast Trail from Gordon River, the woman suddenly lost consciousness. She probably owes her life to the fact that one member of the group had a satellite telephone and was able to place an emergency call. At approximately 10:30 PM the woman was evacuated by boat and then transferred to the hospital by helicopter the next morning.

A Park Warden we met later told us it had been a matter of minutes. The rescue operation had taken place under very difficult circumstances. The rescuer had to risk his own life since the boat was virtually impossible to beach at Thrasher Cove due to heavy wind. A rubber dinghy with a diver had to be put into the water from the rescue boat and the diver had to swim ashore to evacuate the woman.

And another example of how not to do it: A group of German hikers boasted on my last tour that each of them had only 25 (!) granola bars. Overestimation of one's own capabilities and not taking the trail seriously are truly the worst company on the West Coast Trail! If you endanger the lives of others because of foolishness and plain stupidity then you are acting irresponsibly to the highest degree and you should be held accountable!

I mentioned earlier that on my first trip on the West Coast Trail my backpack, and those of the people with me, was too heavy and therefore sheer torture to carry, taking some of the fun out of the trip. They were too heavy because of all the food we carried. Some time later I received a letter from a reader who could not understand why our packs back then had been so heavy. Apparently he had hiked the West Coast Trail with a backpack weighing about 16 kg, including camera equipment. As far as I am concerned, he and his companions were insufficiently equipped and did not carry enough provisions for the trail. Here is why:

In the mid-1990s the small creeks on the trail became raging rivers, impossible to cross, due to very heavy rain. A number of hikers were caught on the trail for 3 days and could not continue on or turn back. Because the stranded hikers carried sufficient food supplies a rescue operation was not necessary.

Everyone should be prepared for such eventualities as well as a few others when hiking the West Coast Trail. Provisions for at least two more days then planned should be included in every backpack.

Hiking on the West Coast Trail has become more and more expensive in recent years. This is not only because of the rising costs of trail maintenance; it is also due to very expensive rescue operations.

In case you are injured so severely that you cannot leave the trail without assistance, follow this procedure:

Included in your trail package is the Accident Information Form. In case of accident or severe injury you have to complete this document and either someone in your party or anyone else you were able to give it to has to bring it to one of the following stations:

- Carmanah or Pachena lighthouse
- Quu'as Trail Guardians (in Tsocowis, Tsuquadra or Camper Bay)
- Trail maintenance crews
- Nitinat Ferry
- Registration and Information Centre at Pachena Bay or Port Renfrew

 Caution! Never leave an injured person behind alone!

The park administration recommends the following safe evacuation points:

Pachena Lighthouse	10 km
Tsocowis Creek	17 km
Tsuquadra Beach	30 km
Nitinat Narrows	32 km
Carmanah Lighthouse	44 km
Walbran Creek	53 km
Logan Creek	56 km
Cullite Creek	58 km
Camper Bay	62 km
Thrasher Cove	70 km

If you are injured, be prepared to wait up to 24 hours before help arrives. The time frame depends entirely on how quickly the Accident Information Form reaches a Park Warden and how far away the Park Warden is from you or the location of the accident.

Of course weather conditions also play a role. A rescue operation by boat or helicopter can be dangerous or even impossible during a storm, fog or rain, etc.

🖐 Attention! The red-white helicopters of the Canadian Coast Guard are not responsible for the evacuation of injured hikers!

If you are injured, try to make yourself visible to the rescuers by waving a towel or drawing attention to yourself. If the rescue operation is by boat, be aware that the boat may not be able to land exactly where you are due to the nature of the coastline. The same applies for rescue by helicopter.

If you happen to have a satellite telephone, you can call the following 24 hour-emergency number for help: 250-726 8035 or, as an alternative: 250-726 7165, Ext. 1. Cellular coverage is *very* sporadic. It may take some time before the call is answered, so let it ring!

TIDE TABLES

Every hiker on the West Coast Trail has to have a tide table and be able to read it. Without a tide table you will likely be surprised when the water floods the beach on which you happen to be hiking and that may prove fatal.

The tide table shows you exactly at what time the tides start and when high or low tide occurs. It is imperative that you are able to read tide tables because the flood water can cut off your path very quickly.

How to read a tide table? Important: The tide table shown opposite is solely for illustration purposes and is NOT valid!

Tide Table 1994 Tofino HNP Z+8

MAY				JUNE			
Day	Time	Ht./ft.	Ht./m	Day	Time	Ht./ft	Ht./m
15	0240	10.3	3.1	1	0015	4.6	1.4
	0930	2.1	0.6		0605	8.7	2.7
SU	1605	9.4	2.9	WE	1220	3.5	1.1
	2135	5.3	1.6		1900	9.9	3.0
16	0325	9.9	3.0	2	0125	4.3	1.3
	1015	2.4	0.7		0720	8.3	2.5
MO	1655	9.3	2.8	THU	1315	4.1	1.2
	2235	5.3	1.6		1950	9.9	3.0
17	0420	9.5	2.9	3	0230	3.8	1.2
	1105	2.7	0.8		0835	8.3	2.5
TU	1745	9.4	2.9	FR	1415	4.4	1.4
	2340	5.1	1.6		2040	10.1	3.1
18	0530	9.1	2.8	4	0325	3.3	1.0
	1200	3.1	0.9		0935	8.5	2.6
WE	1840	9.7	3.0	SA	1505	4.8	1.5
	1200	10.2	3.1				

Day = Date and Day
MO, TU, WE, THU, FR, SA, SU = Monday, Tuesday etc.
Time = local time in 24 hr. format (as calculated from Greenwich Meantime (Z) plus the time difference to local time in hours)
Therefore: 0240 = 2:40 AM local time, 1605 = 4:05 PM local time, 0015 = 12:15 AM local time.
Ht./ft=water level measured in feet
Ht./m=water level measured in metres

For example: On Sunday, May 15, high tide with a high water level measuring 10.3 ft or 3.1 m is at 2:40 AM. Low tide with a water level measuring 2.1 ft or 0.6 m will occur at 9:30 AM.

WEST COAST TRAIL FOR EVERYONE

If you are interested in hiking the West Coast Trail but do not have sufficient time or are not confident that you can manage the entire trail, you can get a taste of the trail on a one- to four-day trip.

It takes one day to hike from Pachena Bay to Pachena Point. If you would like to stay overnight on the trail, you can hike from Pachena Bay to Michigan Creek, Darling River or Tsocowis Creek and then return the next day.

Plan three overnight stays to hike approximately half of the West Coast Trail from Pachena Bay to Nitinat Narrows.

These shorter trips will give you a taste of the lush vegetation, rainforest and the rough and rugged coastal landscape of the West Coast Trail. (Just as a point of information, in 2001 only 3 % of all hikers left the trail at Nitinat Narrows.)

Remember, you still require good and sensible equipment, even if you are only planning a short hike on the West Coast Trail.

WHALE WATCHING

From March to May approximately 20,000 grey whales travel up the West Coast of Vancouver Island. They are on their way from the Baja in Mexico, where their young are born, to their feeding grounds and summer residence, the Bering Sea.

However, a number of them remain in the waters off Vancouver Island, feeding on the fish there. Pacific white-sided dolphins also live here. Besides the grey whales, you can often also see orcas (population approximately 300) as well as humpback whales in the waters around Vancouver Island.

On all of my hikes on the West Coast Trail I have been fortunate enough to spot grey whales from land. Last time, in May, we even watched some orcas. Usually we saw the grey whales from Michigan Creek, the camping spot before you start on your last day's hike. The orcas came into view at about Tsusiat Point.

Of course there is no guarantee that you will see whales. However, I recommend that you keep an eye on the ocean between Tsusiat Point and Michigan Creek during your hike and you may be in luck.

You can recognize whales by the water fountains they blow up when they rise to the surface to breathe. If they are close enough to shore you may even be able to hear them blow.

Discovery Travel Adventure Whale Watching, Nicky Leach and John Gattuso (Editors), ISBN 1563318369, Discovery Communications, 1999

WILDLIFE

Bears

Most bear stories you hear are hugely exaggerated. Especially the media often focus on bears as man-eating monsters. However, the truth is quite different. Bears are actually quite shy and generally avoid humans. There are no grizzlies on Vancouver Island.

The rare encounters with aggressive bears in the past 20 years can usually be attributed to human misbehaviour or error. Wanting to photograph that cute bear cub up close is like attempting suicide since his mother will become a raging beast if anyone or anything gets too close for comfort.

Please report any encounters with bears or bear sighting at the Information Centre when you debrief after your hike!

It rarely happens, but you may run into a black bear on the West Coast Trail. You can obtain information regarding bear activity at the Registration Centre at the trailhead. Notices are usually posted to warn hikers if bears have been seen in a certain area. If you know that bears have been sighted, be especially aware and careful.

There is no need to be afraid as long as you consider and remember a few, common sense rules of conduct. Information brochures with these rules are available to every hiker at the Registration Centres.

Always remember that bears are wild animals. They defend themselves, their offspring and their territory with lightening reflexes when they perceive a threat. Awareness and knowledge of bear behaviour is extremely useful in avoiding a dangerous encounter.

On your hike you should look for signs of bears in the proximity, especially when choosing your camping spot. Tracks, freshly turned soil, cadavers covered with soil and leaves or of course bear-droppings show clearly that a bear is in the vicinity. If you see a bear, do NOT approach him, keep your distance.

Bears feel especially threatened when surprised. Therefore, hiking in groups is advisable, as is whistling, singing or talking loudly. Bear-bells, available in souvenir and outdoor equipment stores, let bears know that you are there. Most bears will leave the area when they notice humans.

Food, garbage or toiletries DO NOT belong in your tent! Bears love soap, toothpaste and other cosmetics. Pack these items in airtight containers and hang them at least 3–4 m up high in the trees. The Park administration has made metal boxes available in some of the camping areas for storing your food etc.

Cook and eat away from your tent – these smells are like an invitation to bears. When you have finished your meal, carry your leftovers and garbage to your storage place between the trees or use the metal boxes provided.

DO NOT bury your garbage! Bears can find buried food and garbage without difficulty and dig it up just as easily. Burning leftovers is also not very effective as you will usually not be able to destroy everything completely.

It has been discovered that bears sometimes react aggressively to menstruating women. Use of tampons is recommended; they should be disposed in airtight plastic bags.

It is illegal to lure animals with food or to feed them. This is for your protection but also for the safety of the animals. Bears remember only too well how and where they were able to get food comfortably.

 If you run into a bear, remember:

- If you see a bear close by, circle around or leave the area. If it approaches you, make loud noise and wave your arms, letting it know you are there. If you cannot retreat, do not panic. Stand still and wait until the bear leaves again – always make sure to leave the bear an escape route.

- Remain calm. Try to evaluate the current situation. Watch the bear's behaviour. Snapping jaws, making a "woof" sound or lowering its head with ears laid back are obvious warning signals. Assume that any bear approaching you like that is ready to attack.

- If a bear rises up on its hind-legs and sucks air through its nostrils, it is attempting to identify its surroundings. Bears cannot see very well, but they have an excellent sense of smell.

- If the bear does not display any aggressive behaviour, speak quietly and gently with it while leaving the scene. Do not run! Bears are as fast as racehorses over short distances. Screaming, hasty movement or running away can cause an immediate attack. Do not throw anything at the bear as this may also provoke an attack.

In case of an attack: Playing dead rarely works. Try to reach a safe place. As a last resort you can attempt to scare the bear away with an object such as your hiking stick or try to fight him off.

In recent years bear spray, which is based on cayenne pepper, has been available in most outdoor equipment stores in Canada and the USA. If you spray a bear with it when he attacks, his eyes and nasal passages will be affected. However, this is no guarantee that the bear will cease attacking. Before you even consider using the spray, make sure you know which way the wind is blowing; otherwise you may have more than one problem!

Over the years I have spoken with a number of different people, park wardens, hikers and ranchers, who survived an attack. They all agreed that bear spray was useful in case of an attack.

Bear spray has one decided advantage for the bear: Pre-bear spray forest workers and park wardens carried firearms for protection. In many cases this resulted in dead bears. Today they often use bear spray instead of a firearm, which means that more bears survive.

It is fascinating to see bears in the wild. Since 'discovering' Canada's wilderness on hiking and canoeing trips, I have had many encounters with bears. Sometimes they were very close to me, as little as 10 m away from where I was, but throughout these years I have not had a single encounter that was even remotely dangerous.

Cougars

The cougar population on Vancouver Island has increased considerably in recent years as it has on BC's mainland. Officially the number of cougars in BC is estimated to be about 4,000. You should therefore be careful.

Cougars are very shy and the likelihood of encountering one is slim, but you should still keep some cautionary measures in mind. Just like bears, cougars are attracted by the smell of food and cosmetics. Using a hiding place in the trees or the metal boxes, when provided, is a good idea.

In late spring to early summer the 2-year old cougar cubs become independent and are away from their mother for the first time. During this time these youngsters wander widely and are also extremely curious. This is when the chance of conflict with humans is the greatest.

Cougar cubs are cute and look very cuddly. HOWEVER, beware those who get too close! Their mother will attack immediately.

Similar to bears, cougars bury their leftover food under soil and leaves. When you recognize such a hiding spot, you should definitely stay away from it because cougars will also defend their food.

In the event of an attack: Wildlife experts advise that you do not turn your back on a cougar but rather look it in the eye, yell at it and try to scare it away with anything at hand – such as your hiking stick – while retreating. If the cougar continues to attack, defend yourself with all you have!

Other Animals

Besides black bears and cougars you may, with a bit of luck, also encounter a number of other animals on the West Coast Trail.

You will probably see bald eagles, whiskey jacks, blue jays, many types of waterfowl and other birds, otters, sea lions, seals as well as grey whales and orcas.

WIND

While it is usually wind-still in the dense rainforest on Vancouver Island, there is usually a stiff breeze blowing on the beach; sometimes it is even stormy. Every hiker on the West Coast Trail should keep that in mind. Especially when hiking along the main part of the trail through the woods, you will perspire a great deal, not least of all due to the exertion when climbing the ladders. Once you leave the forest to continue the hike on the beach, your sweaty body is immediately exposed to the wind and will quickly cool down.

I always experience this as quite pleasant at first, when I finally have the opportunity of hiking on the beach after the strenuous march through the woods. The cooling wind is a welcome refreshment but danger lurks: Hypothermia. (☞ *Hypothermia*) It is important to wear appropriate clothing such as underwear that draws moisture away from the body as well as a windproof fleece sweater or an all-round weather jacket, and, of course, last but not least, a cap or toque to prevent your body from cooling down too quickly and to prevent hypothermia.

CHILL FACTOR

Often ignored, wind chill refers to the temperature you feel at a certain wind velocity rather than what is actually measured. The following table should serve to clarify:

WIND CHILL

Temperature °C	Wind Speed km/h	Felt Temperature °C
14	10	12
	20	6
	30	3
	40	2
10	10	8
	20	3
	30	1
	40	-1
8	10	5
	20	1
	30	-2
	40	-4
6	10	3
	20	-2
	30	-5
	40	-7
4	10	1
	20	-5
	30	-8
	40	-10
2	10	-1
	20	-7
	30	-11
	40	-13
0	10	-4
	20	-10
	30	-14
	40	-16

PORT RENFREW

Port Renfrew, population approximately 280, is located 107 km west of Victoria at the mouth of the San Juan and the Gordon Rivers. Just like the town of Bamfield, the quiet little village is the starting or end point of the West Coast Trail. If you have time, you can also start your excursions to Botanical Beach Provincial Park or the Juan de Fuca Marine Trail. (☞ *Juan de Fuca Marine Trail*). Very few tourists (apart from hikers heading to or from the West Coast Trail) find their way here.

🛏 A German couple, Brigitte and Hans Wasner, run the West Coast Trail Motel, located very close to the Gordon River Trailhead. The Motel offers clean rooms, breakfast as well as a number of other amenities such as a washer and dryer, a large communal living room with a TV and Video recorder. Soaking in the hot tub is a delight after conquering the West Coast Trail. On request transfers can be arranged from here.

> **West Coast Trail Motel**
> Parkinson Road, Port Renfrew, BC
> Tel: 250-647 5565, Fax: 250-647 5566
> Email: wctmotel@islandnet.com

Close to the West Coast Trail Motel is the Lighthouse Pub. Hikers meet here to relax in the comfy atmosphere, exchange experiences of the trail over a beer or two and enjoy a decent meal.

The stages described below represent the daily hike that a hiker in good condition can reasonably be expected to complete. They also allow hikers to enjoy the magnificent and fascinating coastal scenery which would be lost if you were to "zip through" to devour as many kilometers as quickly as possible.

Make sure you pay attention to the current information provided by the staff at the Information and Registration Centres. Take notes.

Hikers in good physical condition can complete the daily stages of the hike, as suggested in this guide, and still have sufficient time to enjoy the spectacular natural environment. Of course you can always hike further, but an important part of the West Coast Trail experience is the rugged coastal landscape and the moderate rainforest – it would be a shame to miss it because you are trying to set speed records; after all, you are not trying to escape.

Please pay attention to the information and advice on trail conditions and wild life provided to hikers by the Registration and Information Centre staff. Make sure you have understood the information, can read the route map and then actually heed the advice or warnings you were given.

Remain on the main trail and only cross surge channels when advised that it is safe to do so. (Alternately, if advised that crossing a surge channel is dangerous, please do NOT cross it!) Surge channels are canals and river mouths with very strong currents and raging water. Minimize risk whenever you can!

INDEX TO THE 7 STAGES

DAY 1
Gordon River to Thrasher Cove   62
See: Route Map 1, p. 63

DAY 2
Thrasher Cove to Camper Creek   70
See: Route Map 1, p. 63

DAY 3
Camper Creek to Logan Creek   74
See: Route Map 2, p. 75

DAY 4
Logan Creek to Cribs Creek   82
See: Route Map 2, p. 75 and Route Map 3, p. 87

DAY 5
Cribs Creek to Tsusiat Falls   91
See: Route Map 3, p. 87 and Route Map 4, p. 95

DAY 6
Tsusiat Falls to Michigan Creek   98
See: Route Map 4, p. 95 and Route Map 5, p. 99

DAY 7
Michigan Creek to Pachena Bay   102
See: Route Map 5, p. 99 and Route Map 6, p. 103

Day 1: Gordon River > Thrasher Cove
☞ **Route Map #1**

The orientation session at the Registration and Information Centre takes approximately 1.5 hours.

Park wardens provide detailed information regarding the trail conditions, current dangers, conditions of the cable cars and ladders, locations of bear and cougar sightings, etc. and then show you a 10 minute video about the West Coast Trail. The movie makes valuable suggestions and gives you a taste of what you can expect on the trail.

Once you have paid your fees for the park, the ferries, etc., you will be issued your official West Coast Trail Pass and are free to start your hike. Make sure you keep the pass with you and in a safe place because it is your ticket for the ferry at Gordon River and again at Nitinat Narrows.

Butch's house is only a short distance from the Registration and Information Centre. He is the ferryman who transfers hikers over the Gordon River to the actual trailhead. The ferry ride takes approximately 5 minutes. His boat leaves at 9 AM, 10:30 AM, 1 PM and 2:30 PM. (See photos opposite and p. 68.)

The trail begins on the other side and you will immediately realize what the West Coast Trail is about. According to the park wardens, the 6 km from the trailhead at Gordon River to Thrasher Cove should take approximately 3 hours. Under optimal trail and weather conditions you may be able to do it that quickly, however, I seriously doubt it.

On my last tour it took us 4.5 hours including a short break. A group of English army reservists who had started their hike just before us took just about as long to complete the same section of the trail.

The trail climbs uphill, seemingly forever, and you will work up quite a sweat. I recommend you take it easy for the first few hours to warm up your body. If your body is not properly warmed up you

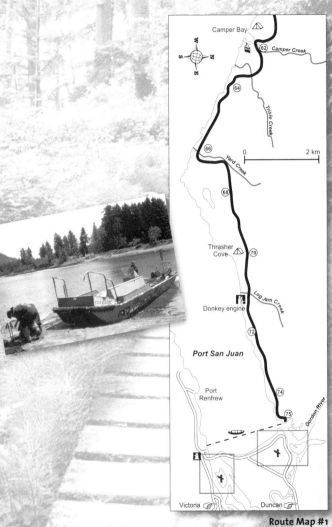

Camper Bay

62 Camper Creek

64

Tistle Creek

66

Yard Creek

0   2 km

68

Thrasher
Cove   70

Log Jam Creek

Donkey engine

72

Port San Juan

74

Port
Renfrew

75
Gordon River

Victoria   Duncan

Route Map #1

risk injuring yourself and it will probably also take a little while before you have adjusted to carrying a backpack.

It was pouring rain and did not look like it was going to improve any time soon when we departed from the West Coast Trail Motel in Port Renfrew at 9 am to head to the Registration Centre at the Gordon River trailhead.

I would not even send out my dog into such weather and here we were, starting our West Coast Trail adventure. Dismal in the truest sense of the word – but, as I knew from previous experience, typical weather for the West Coast Trail.

The park warden at the Registration Centre seemed happy to see us as she gave us very detailed trail information and updates, showed us the trail video and then sent us on our way with a cheery: "Have fun and good luck!"

Originally we had planned to take the 10:30 am ferry across the river to the trailhead but it was raining so hard that this was impossible. We decided to wait a little, have a cup of coffee back at the Motel and hoped that the weather would improve at least a little. By lunchtime it rained a little less and we were driven to the Gordon River ferry where Butch took us over to the trailhead.

The adventure had begun!

The forest is very dense here. That is an advantage because the tree branches are roof-like over your head. The disadvantage? Since everything is damp all the time and not enough sunshine can penetrate through the trees, the trail is always muddy.

Be very careful when hiking over the entangled root systems, because it is almost too easy to slip, stumble and injure yourself.

Then you arrive at the first ladder system! There are 39 of these ladder systems (made up of about 70 individual ladders) on the trail. The longest is approximately 50 m high (either to climb up or down, depending on where you start your hike). Some of the systems have between 5 to 8 ladders. A ladder system consists of a

number of individual ladders interspersed with wooden platforms where you can rest and catch your breath before continuing.

The ladders are extremely challenging! Overcoming the steep coastal cliffs by climbing the ladders while carrying a heavy backpack is sheer torture. You may feel burned out after a very short time, so take your time and allow yourself sufficient rest on the platforms. Remember, you are not in a race!

Stow away your hiking sticks when climbing the ladders otherwise they may get caught in the ladder rungs and end up bent or damaged. It would be a shame to lose them due to simple negligence, as hiking sticks are very practical on the trail. I highly recommend you use hiking sticks, if possible a periscoping set of poles.

✋ Never step in the middle of the rung; it may be too brittle to handle your weight!

The trail continues along the top of the high coastal cliff. However, this does not mean that the path becomes any easier. There are a number of obstacles that impede your way, such as the small canyons that can only be crossed via the enormous trunk of fallen trees that have been cleared of branches and levelled. There are a number of such 'bridges' on the trail. Be extremely careful when walking on these logs, as they are often very slippery.

At km 72, counting from the northern trailhead, is a rusty relic at the edge of the trail that dates back to the time the West Coast Trail was originally built – a donkey engine used to pull tree trunks and boulders. After about one more kilometer you will reach Highest Point, which actually is the highest point of the trail.

🛈 Up to this point the coast has been hidden from view. Here however the forest opens up and you have a spectacular view of the bizarre coastal formations below.

One more kilometer and you reach the turn off to Thrasher Cove. (Difficult to miss since a sign has been posted here.)

▲ From the sign you hike approximately 1 km down the steep coastline until you reach a very long and steep ladder that leads down to the beach. Thrasher Cove is a small bay with a driftwood-covered beach. It is an ideal spot to camp because you can get fresh water from a little creek, however, make sure you pitch your tent above the high tide mark.

After a 4.5-hour hike we finally reached the beach in Thrasher Cove, completely exhausted. It was hard to believe that it had taken us 4.5 hours to hike 6 lousy kilometers, but that is substantial on the West Coast Trail! It was raining a little less. We quickly pitched our tents in a fairly protected spot between piles of driftwood on the beach and then, finally, came the pleasant part of the day. A sumptuous meal made up for the strenuous hike before we crawled into our sleeping bags early that evening.

Thrasher Cove Camp

Ferry crossing Gordon River

Above: Destroyed bridge
Right: Resting on
the beach

Day 2: Thrasher Cove > Camper Creek
☞ **Route Map #1**

Aghast, we stared speechlessly at the 50 m high ladder leading up from Thrasher Cove to the main trail. Very slowly and with many brief breaks we climbed up, rung by painful rung. Our muscles were not yet warmed up properly and we did not want to overexert ourselves that early in the day.

We had woken up around 5:30 am and felt every sore muscle in our weary bodies. The first day and our heavy backpacks had left their mark.

Crawling out of our cosy sleeping bags to stick our heads out of our tents, we were greeted by clammy air and drizzle. A hefty granola breakfast fortified us for the coming day before we broke camp and finally went on our way by 9:15 am.

That ladder, first thing in the morning, was really difficult! Climbing it burned up a lot of our energy. By the time we reached the main trail we were sweat-soaked and had to stop for a breather. However, despite the exertion, the second day seemed somehow easier. Our muscles did not feel as strained and our backpacks had almost become a part of us.

On the previous day we did not really look at the lush rainforest surrounding us. Today however, we consciously experienced it. It was everywhere. Dark green lichen was hanging off the tall Sitka spruce trees. Ferns that grew more than a metre high formed a veil. There were fallen trees, thick roots and swamp plants with large bright green leaves that grew out of marshy puddles. Sparse sunlight penetrated into the thicket and created a fascinating play of shadow and light. It was often difficult to know which way to go in this chaos.

At Thrasher Cove you have two choices:
- You can climb up the long ladder to go back to the turn-off Gordon River/Thrasher Cove and then continue on the main trail to Camper Creek, or
- You can hike along the beach via Owen Point.

☺ The Park administration recommends that hikers use the main trail. If you choose the second route, you must pay attention to the relevant information on the route map:

✋ Caution! The route between Thrasher Cove and Owen Point is only passable when the water level is below 2.40 m. Owen Point itself can only be passed at a water level of less than 1.80 m. Make sure you have checked your tide table and know when it is safe to hike there! This part of the trail is very difficult. On the way, at km 65, you also have to cross a surge channel, which is only possible if the water level is below 1.70 m.

Whenever I hike the West Coast Trail I always follow the advice of the Park administration and recommend other hikers to do the same.

At km 66 on the main trail you will arrive at the first long board-walk system. It winds through the forest for approximately 2 km with few interruptions and allows you to walk quite comfortably. Still, be careful! The boardwalks are extremely slippery when it is raining or when they are wet.

The hike between km 64 and the campsite at Camper Creek is strenuous. Camper Creek must be crossed by cable car.

We arrived at Camper Creek, our destination that day, by 4:00 pm.

It had taken us 6 hours and 45 minutes to hike the mere 7 km from Thrasher Cove to Camper Creek! Our second day had also been quite a challenge and we had to rest fairly often.

At Camper Creek we encountered a mode of transport hitherto unknown to us – a cable car. A primitive cableway led across the wide but flat riverbed of Camper Creek. Each one of us pulled himself and his backpack across to the other side where we put up camp. It was not raining, but the sky was shrouded in dark clouds. Quite a muggy atmosphere!

We had difficulty lighting a fire because firewood was sparse and the little we were able to find was damp. Finally the flames started to dance and we immediately felt a bit more comfortable despite the weather.

After an extensive meal and many cups of tea we briefly investigated our surroundings before crawling into our sleeping bags and falling into a deep sleep almost immediately.

Tree bridge between Thrasher
Cover and Camper Creek

Day 3: Camper Creek > Logan Creek
☞ Route Map #2

*The rain was drumming on the roof of our tent. Sleepily I crept out
of my sleeping bag and opened the tent flap. Raindrops hit my face.
The clouds were hanging low. The wind was pushing thick veils of rain
across the landscape. Filthy weather!*

*I recalled my first hike on the West Coast Trail. The weather back
then at Camper Creek had been equally bad. Then as now we decided
to wait a while to see how the weather would develop. There is nothing
quite as nice as staying in your cosy sleeping bag when the morning
outside is so ugly!*

*By 11:00 am we were ready to go. It was still raining heavily when we
headed out after our morning ablutions and a fortifying breakfast to
hike to Logan Creek.*

The next 6 km are very intense. It is basically a day of ladders and
mud! The longest ladder system of the hike, 8 ladders, is at Cullite
Creek.

It takes a while to cross the Cullite Creek valley. The creek itself has to be crossed by cable car and, once on the other side, you
have to climb a number of ladders to get to the top of the steep
cliff.

*The rain-covers for our backpacks were indispensable in this miserable
weather. The rain made the forest seem like a hothouse.*

*The air was damp and big drops of condensed water fell from the
trees. The trail itself was swampy and even wetter than on the
previous day.*

*Once we were in the forest we did not notice the rain so much,
but instead became very conscious of being sweat-soaked. The many
ladders on this stretch proved to be quite a challenge. We experienced
our 'ladder-climax' at Cullite Creek. At first, a 50 m long ladder system
descended almost vertically down the steep cliff to Cullite Creek.*

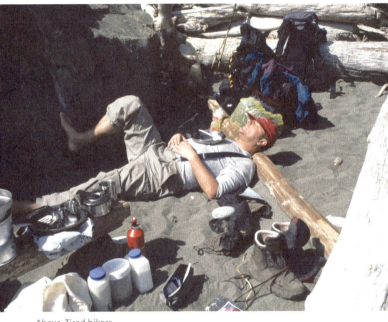

Above: Tired hikers
Left: Shower under Tsusiat Falls

Climbing down was fairly easy and crossing the creek by cable car also went smoothly, but climbing the ladder system up the cliff on the other was harrowing!

Once we reached the top, we had to break for a few minutes before we were able to continue our hike. The long boardwalk that followed offered a little respite for our ladder-weary bones.

▲ Just before crossing Cullite Creek, a trail turns off the main path to a camping spot by the ocean.

Walking the long boardwalk after Cullite Creek is quite comfortable. However, afterwards it gets a bit muddy. The trail is partially submerged under large, knee-deep mud puddles. To keep your feet reasonably dry, good gaiters – Gore-Tex is great – are essential for this part of the trail. It is slow going through here.

▲ The destination of the day, Logan Creek, is reached by climbing down one more long ladder system. The space here is limited, but somehow you can always find a spot for your tent.

We finally arrived at Logan Creek at 4:30 pm after climbing down, for the last time that day, a very long ladder system.

A five and a half hour hike was behind us. Not exactly a great feat compared to a 'normal' hike. But besides the many ladder systems our path was complicated by many muddy stretches, which had slowed us down considerably.

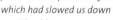

Campsite at Logan Creek

Bonilla Point

Memories of times gone by

Day 4: Logan Creek > Cribs Creek
☞ Route Maps #2 and #3

The mouth of Logan Creek is long and narrow. Steep and thickly treed cliffs rise up on both sides of it. You must cross it via a narrow, adventurous-looking suspension bridge up in dizzying heights.

The bridge is absolutely safe to cross even though it swings back and forth quite a bit, which may make your stomach feel slightly queasy as you are walking across. The main trail leads over this bridge.

✋ Although it is possible to continue along the beach from Logan Creek, it is highly recommended that you use the main trail. Should you still consider hiking along the beach, beware of the Adrenaline Creek surge channel at km 55. Crossing it is rated as extremely dangerous by the Park administration.

To get to the suspension bridge crossing Logan Creek you will have to climb back up a ladder system that leads out of the Logan Creek valley.

As on the previous day, many ladders and mud govern the speed at which you progress. Use extreme when climbing over fallen tree trunks. The trunks are usually very slippery due to the moisture in the air and sometimes there is no way around, especially on the stretch between Camper and Walbran Creeks.

Walbran Creek is at km 53. It is a little tricky to wade across the creek at high tide. Watch out for the dangerous currents and try to cross as close to the ocean as you can. Hiking sticks come in handy here to help maintain your balance.

▲ The route map does not show an official campground at Walbran Creek, but it is a very beautiful tenting spot.

From Walbran Creek you can continue along the beach but be sure you have checked the tide table and are aware of the water level while walking there. Vancouver Point is passable only at a water level below 2.70 m.

☺ Hiking along the beach can be very pleasant compared to the very challenging passages on the main trail – if you know where to walk. Walking in the soft dry sand is difficult because you sink in due to the combined weight of you and your backpack. However, if you walk where the water has washed over the beach and the beach has not quite dried, the sand is more compact and you will not sink in as much.

📷 Up to now, because of the thick bush, the glimpses of the coastal scenery have been few and far between – but now, on the beach after Walbran Creek, the magnificent landscape stretches out before you. To the right is the steep rocky cliff with trees growing on top of it. Along the beach bizarre rock formations, some as high as houses, sculpted by the wind and weather of the Pacific Ocean, reach up to the sky. Mounds of driftwood line the beach.

🚩 Shortly after km 50 you step onto First Nations property. There are six First Nations Reserves along the entire trail. This is private property and every hiker should respect that.

⛺ Carmanah Creek at km 46 has to be crossed by cable car. You can tent here between the mounds of driftwood; it is marked as an official campground on the route map.

🚩 Between km 46 and 44 you are again on First Nations property.

Just a few hundred metres before you reach the Carmanah Lighthouse at km 44, built to aid ships in this treacherous coastal region, you come upon what any hiker least expects to find on the West Coast Trail – believing himself to be in pristine wilderness:

Chez Monique

☺ Chez Monique, a Kiosk or mini-restaurant, is run by a First Nations couple. It is utterly surprising and odd to come upon something like this here but nevertheless, you will find everything your exhausted hiker's heart desires. Great hamburgers and lovely, cool beer – but not cheap!

Cable car at Carmanah Creek

The 16 kilometers between Logan Creek and Cribs Creek make up the longest stretch of the trail, but once you have passed Carmanah Lighthouse, it is fairly easy going since the main trail to Cribs Creek is in good condition and you can hike it at a brisk pace.

𝗔 The camping spot at Cribs Creek (see photograph, p. 89) is one of the most beautiful on the entire trail. It is located directly at the mouth of the creek. Tents may be pitched on either side of the creek.

We broke camp at Logan Creek at 8:30 am and headed out to hike the 16 kilometers to Cribs Creek. After crossing the suspension bridge over Logan Creek, the West Coast Trail continued to challenge us for the first half of the day: Ladders and lots and lots of mud!

Once we reached Walbran Creek at 10:30 am that changed. From here on we were able to continue our hike, for the first time, along the beach. However, before we could continue on, we had to cross Walbran Creek, which seemed difficult. For one thing, the creek further up from its mouth was very wide and deep and for another, there was a very strong current close to the mouth.

We took a break, ate something, let our sweat-soaked and mud-covered clothes dry in the sun and discussed how we would get across without risking life or limb – or taking a bath.

The weather had improved. When we left Logan Creek it had been raining, now we felt blessed by the warm sunshine.

We ended up crossing the creek using our hiking sticks. Even though the water reached over our knees and pulled strongly at our legs all of us made it to the other side safely, without a bath.

Once there, we hiked for a long while along the beach and reached Chez Monique at about 4:00 pm. We enjoyed hamburgers and a beer before continuing on our way an hour later. By 6:30 pm we arrived at Cribs Creek.

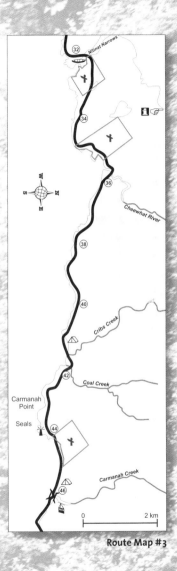

Route Map #3

Driftwood

Camp spot at Cribs Creek

Ferry at Nitinat Narrows

Day 5: Cribs Creek > Tsusiat Falls
☞ Route Maps #3 and #4

From Cribs Creek you have the option of either following the main trail or travelling along the beach.

🖐 Another difficult surge channel is located at km 38. This surge channel can only be crossed when the water level is below 2.10 m. It is possible to avoid the surge channel by going onto the main trail once you have passed Daure Point.

🏔 The main trail follows along the edge of the cliff at a dizzying height, but the view is spectacular. Below are romantic and isolated small bays. The cliffs have been eroded by the breakers from the Pacific Ocean, which continually batter the coast. The scenery is so bizarre, untamed and wild that it is difficult to describe with mere words.

🖐 To reach Nitinat Narrows you have to follow the trail leads back into the forest. The boardwalks here are treacherous, often rotten and therefore brittle, so be extremely cautious and careful.

✝ Between km 36 and 34 as well as between km 33 and 32 you are once again on First Nations land.

The Nitinat Narrows are a true obstacle for West Coast Trail hikers. It is impossible to wade or swim across because the currents in the estuary are so strong that it is dangerous to cross even by boat.

The Park administration has organised a ferry service operated by the First Nations in Nitinat Village. Once you have shown your official West Coast Trail Pass you will be ferried across.

🖐 The ferry service is offered daily until 4:00 or 5:00 PM. Plan to be there by about 3:00 PM to make sure you will be ferried across.

Ferry at Nitinat Narrows

☺ If you do not want to hike the entire West Coast Trail you can leave the trail at Nitinat Narrows (☞ *Getting there* and ☞ *West Coast Trail for Everyone*).

🛈 At first, you have to follow the main trail from Nitinat Narrows up to km 31, but from here you may continue along the beach. The view from the top of the cliffs over the rocky coastline with the thundering surf is stunning.

🐦 Keep a look out to the ocean for seals and sea lions between km 31 and Michigan Creek. They can often be seen on the rocky promontories and sometimes you may even see some grey whales swim by as well.

🛉 You will again be on First Nations land between km 31 and 29.

Tsusiat Point, the rock with the hole in it, is visible from far away. Here, at km 28, the surging waters of the Pacific Ocean have 'eaten' a 5 m wide by 3 m high hole through a large rock formation that sticks out into the sea. It is an imposing natural edifice.

Tsusiat Point can only be passed at a water level of less than 2.70 m. It is possible to go around on the main trail, but then you will miss seeing many of the scenic attractions such as Tsusiat Point.

You can hike along the beach all the way to Tsusiat Falls. There is a lake northeast of the trail called Tsusiat Lake. A river of the same name runs through the lake on its way down to the Pacific Ocean. It is wide and sluggish as it winds through the rainforest but at km 25 it turns into a 10 metres high and 12 metres wide spectacular waterfall. The large amount of water collects in a crystal clear pool before flowing into the ocean.

Tsusiat Falls is definitely one of the main attractions on the West Coast Trail. The magnificent waterfall is the focal point of this idyllic long bay, which also boasts with a fine gravel and sand beach and incredible amounts of driftwood.

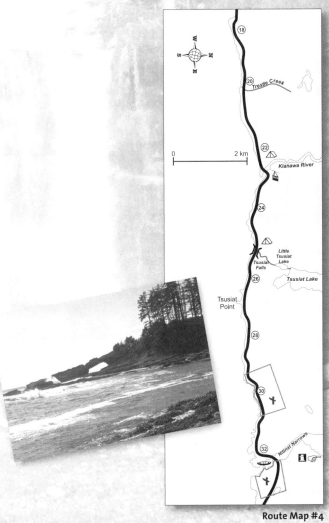

18

20 Trestle Creek

W N
S E

0 ___ 2 km

22
Klanawa River

24

Little
Tsusiat
Lake

Tsusiat
Falls

26
Tsusiat Lake

Tsusiat
Point

28

30

Nitinat Narrows

32

i

Route Map #4

Above: Tsusiat Falls camp
Right: Tide pool at
Michigan Creek

At 9:30 am we headed out from Cribs Creek to Tsusiat Falls, our desti-nation for that day. The weather had grown worse again and we had to break camp in the rain – always an unpleasant experience. The tent is saturated with water and therefore heavy and it is difficult to shake off the wet sand.

But that would not to ruin our day. We really enjoyed hiking through the magnificent wilderness that surrounded us. Sometimes we hiked on the beach and sometimes we chose to walk along the edge of the cliff, relishing the breathtaking view of the coastline from up there.

While we carefully navigated the brittle boardwalk on the main trail at approximately km 38, I once again recalled my first trip on the West Coast Trail. I had slipped on one of these treacherous boardwalks and pulled a muscle in my thigh, a very painful experience I definitely did not wish to repeat.

We arrived at Nitinat Narrows at 2:00 pm and were ferried across after enjoying a refreshing ice tea we were able to purchase there. Once on the other side, we continued on the main trail, over many board-walks and through a lot of mud to km 28, where we went down to the beach to continue the hike. On a few of the outlying rocks in the ocean we discovered seals and a few sea lions.

We noticed our first whales when we heard them breathe and then saw the water fountains their breath sent up out of the water at Tsusiat Point. The tide was already starting to come in and we just made it through the 'gateway,' the hole in the rock. We reached Tsusiat Falls, our destination for the day, at approximately 6:00 pm. The weather was actually quite nice. Between the mountains of driftwood we found a protected spot for our tent and settled in for the evening. Just before turning in for the night I took a quick shower underneath the waterfall.

Be warned: The water is freezing cold!

Day 6: Tsusiat Falls > Michigan Creek
☞ Route Maps #4 and #5

Starting at Tsusiat Falls the main trail again winds through the rainforest. It is impossible to continue hiking along the beach. However, in order to reach the main trail, you have to conquer a very steep and long ladder system from the beach to the top of the cliff.

🛈 The view from there is grandiose as the coastline below is rough and breathtakingly beautiful.

The next but also the last big obstacle on the West Coast Trail is the Klanawa River. The wide and slow-running river has to be crossed by cable car.

From Klanawa River to Trestle Creek the route once again follows the beach. From there, at km 20, you have to return to the main trail again to reach Tsocowis Creek. At Trestle Creek, exactly where the way to the main trail is marked, is an old rusty anchor dating back to the time of the shipwrecks.

Along the way, you will pass two more relics dating back to the time the West Coast Trail was built, a donkey engine and a grader.

Valencia Bluffs, at km 18, is the spot where the steamship *Valencia* sank in a storm on January 22, 1906. That shipwreck was one of the reasons the West Coast Trail was built.

Tsocowis Creek cascades down the high cliff to the ocean shore. A very pretty wooden bridge spans the creek.

A few metres further down you may want to turn onto a steep path down to the beach, away from the main trail. Looking back to the creek from the beach, you get a great view of the bridge.

🛈 If you walk back along the beach from Tsocowis Creek to km 17, you will see Billy Goat Creek turn into a high and narrow waterfall as it rushes down the cliff.

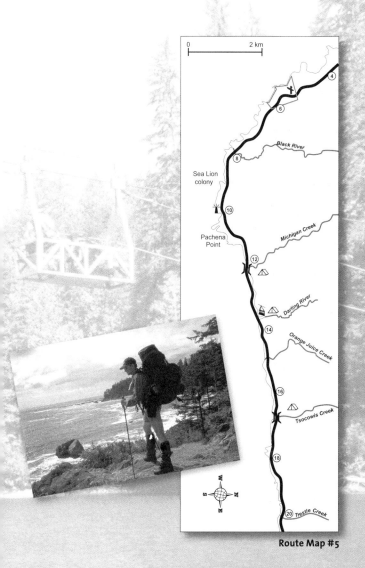

0   2 km

4

6

Black River

8

Sea Lion
colony

10

Michigan Creek

Pachena
Point

12

Darling River

14

Orange Juice Creek

16

Tsocowis Creek

18

N
W   E
S

20   Trestle Creek

Route Map #5

The rusty remains of a shipwreck rest at km 16, reminding hikers once again of past tragedies.

You can only hike along the beach to km 15 if the water level is 2.70 m or less. Pay close attention to the route map as well as the tide table!

Darling River may be crossed by cable car, but you can also wade across if the water level is about mid-level.

🛖 There is a campground at Darling River.

On the coast between Darling River and Michigan Creek are many flat, wide tide pools teeming with life. Especially birds like seagulls take advantage of this rich food source.

You can see a lot of different species in the many rocky crags and niches that are often covered with algae. Starfish as big as plates and countless water plants add to the colourful mix (see photograph, p. 96).

The hike between Tsusiat Falls and Michigan Creek is about 13 kilometers long, fairly easy and one of the prettiest sections of the trail with a great chance to see whales.

At km 12, Michigan Creek, hikers that started from the south pitch their tent for the last time before they finish their hike.

We were woken up by rain. What am I saying, rain? It was pouring cats and dogs and the rain drummed onto out tents. No one felt like getting up to prepare breakfast.

However, a little later I forced myself to get up, slipped into my rain gear and zipped open the tent. It was not only raining, it was also quite chilly.

I quickly made tea and prepared some granola and after a while I did not care about the rain anymore. You can get used to anything, especially rain, if you happen to be hiking the West Coast Trail.

At 10:20 am we were ready to go. As usual, climbing the steep ladder up to the main trail was very challenging, but we took it easy and did not push ourselves too hard. Boardwalks and mud alternated with spectacular vistas spread out before us and ensured we were not bored on our way to Klanawa River.

After crossing the Klanawa River by cable car we had to balance over mountains of driftwood in order to get to the beach to continue our hike. It reminded me of Mikado, a game played with wooden sticks.

Between Tsocowis Creek and Michigan Creek we witnessed a unique spectacle of nature: A pod of grey whales was swimming along the coast, very close to shore, looking for food. We took our time and watched them for a while.

We reached Michigan Creek at 5:00 pm and pitched our tent for the last time. And, how could it be otherwise, on our second to last day the weather improved. Although the sky was still partially obscured by a few towering cumulus clouds, the sun was smiling down on us.
Two bald eagles were spiralling above us. Presumably their nest was in the vicinity, here in the trees around Michigan Creek. We had frequently observed them over the last few days and admired their majestic air.

After a sumptuous meal, we sat back, relaxed by the fire and enjoyed a romantic sunset. We looked out over the ocean and in the fading sunlight we could see a number of grey whales appear sporadically. In the dusky silence we clearly heard them snorting out water from their blowhole, we saw the water fountains and when they dove into the deep, their tailfins were silhouettes on the glowing horizon.
It was a magnificent spectacle that will stay in our memory long after completing the West Coast Trail.

Day 7: Michigan Creek > Pachena Bay
☞ Route Maps #5 and #6

The last stretch of the trail, between Michigan Creek and Pachena Bay, again winds through the rainforest. The last 12 kilometers are easy to hike and quite harmless when compared to earlier days.

Two kilometers into the hike you reach Pachena Point. A lighthouse was built here after the shipwreck of the SS *Valencia*. It is still in operation. When the weather is bad and everything is shrouded fog you can hear the lonesome hooting of the foghorn for miles. An inviting picnic table awaits at the edge of the steep cliff where the lighthouse property ends. The people who run the lighthouse sell homemade fudge and small souvenirs. You can also get fresh water here for the remainder of your hike.

🐦 On the rocks below the cliff, approximately one kilometer past Pachena lighthouse is a large sea lion colony. If you follow the main trail, you have to cross two bridges after Pachena Point. Shortly afterwards a narrow trail leads toward the coast. If you would like to see the sea lions, follow the trail through thick brush and after 100 metres you will arrive at the edge of the cliff and have an excellent view of the sea lions on the rocks below.

The gigantic trees and lush vegetation on the last kilometers of the trail to Pachena Bay once again impress with the magnificence of the rainforest. Take your time here and soak up the purity surrounding you before you head back to civilisation....

If you started from Port Renfrew, Pachena Bay, a wide bay with a beautiful huge sandy beach, is the end of your West Coast Trail experience.

You may ask yourself why I choose to start my hikes from Port Renfrew rather than from Pachena Bay. The stretch from Pachena Bay to Walbran Creek is doubtless the easier route for hikers with a heavy

*backpack when compared to the very difficult and strenuous stretch
from Port Renfrew.*

*However, I will probably always prefer Port Renfrew as my starting
point because I like getting the difficult and challenging part out of the
way in order to then really enjoy the (in my opinion) most beautiful
part of this challenging hike. Once you found your rhythm on the first
part and your backpack is a little lighter when you reach Walbran
Creek, you are free to really experience the second portion of the West
Coast Trail.*

Debriefing at the Registration and Information Centre in Pachena
Bay is a necessary formality and very quick.

⛺ Tenting is permitted on the magnificent Pachena Bay beach. I
consider it a lovely end to the trip to stay here over night one last
time and reminisce on the events of the hike. If your time permits
and the weather plays along, you should definitely try it.

*On our last day we decided to hike from Michigan Creek to Pachena
Point without breakfast because we wanted to breakfast at the lighthouse. From earlier West Coast Trail experiences I knew of the picnic
table in the garden surrounding the lighthouse and thought it would
be a fitting site for our last breakfast on the trail.*

*The weather was excellent that morning, so we broke camp and
headed out at 7:15 am. Just over half an hour later we sat beneath the
lighthouse in glorious sunshine and enjoyed the view as well as an
extensive breakfast.*

*Afterwards we went to the viewpoint to see some sea lions, but there
was only one huge sea lion lying on the rocks below. We shouldered our
backpacks for the last time and hiked through the thick, damp rainforest to Pachena Bay.*

*Along the way we met up with a number of small groups that were
just heading out on the trail from Pachena Bay. Their clothing still
looked crisp and clean. We however looked like anyone who has hiked
the West Coast Trail – grimy!*

Pachena Bay Registration Center

BAMFIELD

Bamfield, the heart of Pacific Rim National Park, is a small, dreamy village of about 300 souls, located on the south side of Barkley Sound. There is not a lot of tourism here but the terrain is quite interesting for sport fishers, kayakers, whale watchers and hikers. Fishermen and artists that have succumbed to the attraction of this remote spot on Vancouver Island live in quaint, pretty houses. There are a number of small hotels and Bed & Breakfasts that offer accommodation at reasonable cost. Some parts of the village can only be reached by boat.

Bamfield is the starting or end point for West Coast Trail hikers. The village is located approximately 5 kilometers from the trailhead at Pachena Bay.

☺ If you like, you can hike the Cape Beale Trail from Bamfield in addition to the West Coast Trail. The Cape Beale trailhead is located just south of Bamfield and leads to Keeha Beach or rather the Cape Beale lighthouse, approximately 10 kilometers away. The Cape Beale Trail is shown on the West Coast Trail route map.

Accommodation/Activities in Bamfield

🛏 Imperial Eagle Lodge & Charters
Tel: 250-728 3430

🛏 Marie's B&B
Tel: 250-728 3091

🛏 Mill's Landing Cottages & Charters
Tel: 250-728 2300

🛏 Tide's Inn B&B
Tel: 250-728 3376

🛏 Bamfield Trail Motel
Tel: 250-728 3231

🚐 ⚠ Centennial Park/Campground
Tel: 250-728 3006

🎣 🚐 ⚠ Seabeam Fishing Resort/Campground
Tel: 250-728 3286

🛶 Bamfield Kayak Centre
Tel: 250-728 3535

🛏 🎣 Bamfield's Tyee Resort & Fishing Lodge
Tel: 250-728 3296

🐋 🛶 Broken Island Adventures
Tel: 250-728 3500

🛏 McKay Bay Lodge
Tel: 250-728 3323

☺ And then there is of course Hawk's Nest Pub with its cosy atmosphere and excellent fish & chips.

I WISH ALL READERS who decide to hike the West Coast Trail a beautiful and adventurous trip without accidents, injuries or mishaps.

Hiking the West Coast Trail is an unforgettable experience. You will sweat, curse and wonder what possessed you to want to hike the trail, but hopefully, the breathtaking scenery and the pristine natural environment will also fascinate you. And then, when you are sitting by the fire in the evening after a strenuous day, sipping on a cup of hot tea or cocoa while listening to the ocean, you may realize that this is the experience of a lifetime, well worth the effort. Good luck – have a great and safe trip!

Pachena Point

INDEX

Accident Information Form	45	First Nations	20, 83, 91, 94
Adrenaline Creek	82		
Alberni Marine Services	33	Gordon River	62
Backpack cuisine	22	Highest Point	66
Bears	49	Hypothermia	36
Bamfield	32, 106		
Bannock	23	Information & Registration Centres	37
Billy Goat Creek	98	Injuries	37
Boardwalk	15		
Cable car	16, 71, 98, 100	Juan de Fuca Marine Trail	38
Camper Creek	71		
Cape Beale Trail	106	Kiosk	85
Carmanah Creek	83	Klanawa River	98
Carmanah lighthouse	83		
Chill factor	54	Ladder system	64, 74, 98
Cougars	52	Logan Creek	78, 82
Cribs Creek	86		
Cullite Creek	74	Michigan Creek	100, 102
Darling River	100	Nitinat Narrows	35, 91
Daure Point	91	Nitinat Village	35, 91
Donkey engine	66		
Driftwood	88, 94	Opening hours	38
Drinking water	26, 67	Owen Point	71
Emergency	42	Pachena Bay	102
Equipment	16	Pachena Bay Trailhead	104
		Port Alberni	32
Food	22	Port Renfrew	59
Fee	41		
Ferry	29, 33, 34, 91	Qualicum Beach	31

Red tide   37
Reservation system   39
Recipes   22

Safety   42
Sea lions   94, 102
Shipwrecks   100
Surge channels   60, 71, 82, 91
Suspension bridge   82

Thrasher Cove   66, 70
Tide pools   100
Tide table   46
Trestle Creek   98
Tsocowis Creek   98
Tsusiat Falls   94, 98
Tsusiat Point   94

Valencia Bluffs   9, 98
Vancouver   27
Vancouver Island   29
Vancouver Point   83
Victoria   30

Walbran Creek   82
West Coast Trail Express   32
Whales   31, 48, 97
Wildlife   49
Wind   54

Also published by Positive Connections Ltd:
Outdoor Guide: Bowron Lakes

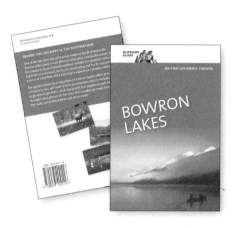

Available at your local bookstore or online at:
www.outdoorguidebooks.net

We look forward to your comments, corrections,
additions, questions or book orders. To contact
us please send an email to:
info@outdoorguidebooks.net

Positive Connections Ltd.
411–1490 Pennyfarthing Drive
Vancouver, BC
V6J 4Z3, Canada